BLACK PIONEERS

BLACK

Images of the Black Experience

THE UNIVERSITY OF UTAH PRESS   *Salt Lake City*

John W. Ravage

PIONEERS

on the North American Frontier

Library of Congress Cataloging-in-Publication Data

Ravage, John W.
Black pioneers : images of the Black experience on the
North American Frontier / John W. Ravage
p.   cm.
Includes bibliographical references (p.   ) and index.
ISBN 0-87480-546-5 (cloth : alk. paper)
1. Afro-American pioneers—West (U.S.)—History—Pictorial works.
2. Frontier and pioneer life—West (U.S.)—Pictorial works.
3. West (U.S.)—History—Pictorial works.
I. Title.
E185.925.R38   1997
978'.00496073—dc21
97-33416

Frontispiece: Sam McCullough, Jr. and the Battle of Goliad from Texas' Revolution. Reputedly, his was the first blood shed in the Texas war for liberation from Mexico. Photo of stained glass window in Texas State Capitol Building. Source: Institute for Texan Cultures, San Antonio.

For Chris and Jeff, two sons of whom I am immensely proud . . .

. . . and as a partial answer to the actor, William Marshall,
who asked me some thirty years ago,
"And what are you doing about racial issues in our society?"

CONTENTS

FOREWORD

As we embark upon the twenty-first century, W. E. B. DuBois's prophetic analysis of the *color line* seems ever more apparent and practical. He was addressing the dilemma of African diasporic people being dismissed, aborted, and placed on the margins of world history and, more importantly, Americana history. Equally important, regional and community studies are the ontological base in which one can begin to examine the historical and cultural experiences of blacks throughout the diaspora. Moreover, DuBois, like Carter. G. Woodson and Charles H. Wesley, to name a few, were African American historians, who consistently pointed to issues and schema of historiography, with emphasis on interpretative analysis, method, and theoretical application. Hence, their research was thorough, accurate, and preserved a legacy for an intellectual tradition of academic rigor and critical analysis. In contemporary times, scholars who study the African diasporic historical and cultural experiences, are challenged with the task to transform consciousness, transcend scholarly rigor, while simultaneously seeking to provide an alternative epistemological framework to query, describe, and evaluate Africana phenomena.

Indeed, the pursuit of addressing an alternative view is paradoxical. Much of this is reflective of the ideological repertoire and philosophical location of the author. Ironically, African-American studies scholars are confronted with the dilemma of re-conceptualizing memory and ethos of black diasporic regional and community studies, in the way of tracing signposts and maps, that are retentative variables within the African cultural continua. Even more important, within this intellectual methodological sojourn to critically examine Africana history and culture, there is a pattern; whereas, a majority of the studies on black diasporic communities have been too descriptive, lacking any assessment of cultural relativity and retention of African culture.

Thus, Jack Ravage, has made a significant contribution to the intellectual history of African diasporic regional studies. His emphasis primarily is focused on presenting aesthetics, in the form of photographs, of the African diasporic presence in the American frontier, Canada, Alaska, and Hawaii. His interdisciplinary approach of studying this presence queries social historiography vindication of a continual pattern of black subordination and oppression. Still, not providing a narration of this book, it is imperative to explain in a general sketch, yet, informative context, how African diasporic people have maintained and demonstrated tenacity in their attempt to locate a niche in the public and economic sphere of Americana society. Variables such as culture, politics, and social life are key tools of analysis used in this study by the author in order to develop a contextual foundation of African diasporic historiography.

Accordingly, this task is rigorous. However, Ravage pursues the subject matter with clarity, breadth, and depth, concerning the limitations, validity, and particular focus of the subject matter. In fact, the thematic schema extracted within the body of this book describe and evaluate multiple articulations of the black experiences in the areas of housing, employment, politics, education, economics, and social issues.

Ravage's pictorial history employs tools of analysis within the social sciences and humanities. His perspective and views are fresh and creative. He acknowledges his intersubjective bias as a European American attempting to study Africana kinship and culture. Also, Ravage addresses the interpersonal conflicts of examining African diasporic people as subjects, reflective of their own historical and cultural experiences, and not as objects. Again, this point is essential and key. He explicitly points out the problems of white scholars imposing their views and values in assessing and defining the aesthetic dimensions of black culture. Unequivocally, this articulates and implies that a "shared authority" has been employed in this study. Furthermore, Ravage's qualitative assessment of African diasporic people in the American West, Canada, Alaska, and Hawaii provides a deep structural analysis to locate retentions of Africana culture and memory.

In closing, Jack Ravage has produced a prolific work, studying Africana people as they moved westward and northward in a land to which they or their elder family members had been brought as slaves. Appropriately, he has invaded the sphere of presenting *"cutting-edge"* scholarship, in the way of examining variables within a historical context. Yet, the challenge and quest of this book exemplifies rigor. In addition, the essential challenge of this book, is that forthcoming scholars employ a "new theory" on community-regional studies to explain, enumerate, and develop a contextual analysis of African diasporic people in the North American continent and Hawaii in place, space, and time.

James L. Conyers, Jr.
Chair, Department of Black Studies
The University of Nebraska at Omaha

PREFACE

After the end of institutionalized slavery with the signing of the Emancipation Proclamation near the close of the Civil War, profound changes took place in the living patterns of African American citizens of the United States and parts of Canada. That most individuals chose to remain in the South, staying in former slave states to live and work as free men and women, was not surprising. Some emigrated to northern areas to seek jobs and opportunities that had been denied them regarding educational, social, and political development. (Two generations later, European immigrants would arrive in those same areas.) Far fewer would move to the American and Canadian West—the new territories of the time.

Migration of North Americans has been part and parcel of their historical longings for freedom, expansion, opportunity, and economic betterment. To this day, people mythologize the importance of the western

(left) The man in this photograph, described as "Chief of the Shirashep," is actually Clifford Hancock, a civilian employee of the U.S. military dressed as a fanciful "Black Eskimo." Taken in Alaska in 1899, this image is an indication of the increasing influence of African Americans in that northern region. (Courtesy of the Rasmussen Collection, University of Alaska Archives, Fairbanks)

movement in literature, films, and popular entertainment, but those presentations are often the stuff of dreams, not reality. The fantasy world of "the West" is one filled with strong, durable men and women, the sons and daughters of European forebears. In this fantasy scenario, however, African Americans and other minority groups seem tacked on as merely added dramatic personae who—while they may occasionally fill out the subplots—seldom grace the main action.

As with much of recorded history, it was not that way at all.

This book intends to reveal how African American pioneers in the greater North American West, including Alaska, have been systematically overlooked or excluded from the predominant social history for a variety of political, emotional, and cultural reasons, which were—and are—not founded on fact. Through photographs and other graphic images of these pioneers and their work and experiences, their historical presence is revealed in a broad range of laborers, professionals, builders, gamblers, roughnecks, politicians, leaders, followers, good men and women—bad ones, too—who were the same in all respects as other men and women with the stamina and drive required to face a hostile environment. They were the same except for the color of their skin. Most were simply hardworking human beings who sought for themselves a secure future, nothing more.

For the illustrations that follow, my intention was to collect images and profiles of the rich and poor, good and bad, young and old, man and woman, Godly and Godless. All this, so that part of the record of those earlier times may document that the residents of western North America and Alaska were truly a tumbled mix of racial heritages, philosophies, and accomplishments.

In order to research and assemble all of the material, I traveled to and examined over fifty collections and corresponded with curators of at least fifty others. Although much of the material was found in archives ranging from small museum and library collections to major holdings in state, provincial, and educational institutions, other valuable sources were private, individual collections and, literally, dozens of small and large collections residing in out-of-the-way places. (See List of Collections.)

For the illustrations I have included not only items seldom found in print but also those that—while more commonly seen—are the only known images of some individuals. Yet, to leave out the more familiar representations would create an incomplete and misleading list. In making my selections it was a fine line to walk. Many of the illustrations included exist, for all intents and purposes, in no other printed form or in publications with a small circulation. All in all, they present a "new look" at evidence of individuals of African descent in western United States and Canada and Alaska whose existance has gone unnoticed.

Without substantial research aid from the University of Wyoming's Department of Communication and Mass Media (and unremitting support from Chair Frank Millar) as well as Michael Devine and Richard Ewig of the American Heritage Center at the University of Wyoming and a Research Grant from the University of Wyoming, none of this work could have been accomplished. Special appreciation is extended to Melinda Bobo for her skills in copy editing, proofing, and indexing.

Most important, the constant support of Linda Ravage, my wife, made the project achievable and enjoyable.

Minor obstacles to research arose because racial issues still elicit strong emotions to this day and are often barriers to collecting information about ethnic groups.

While this book is not intended to be the seminal work on the subject, neither is it devoted solely to "important" African Americans of the era. Such an approach would indicate a massive conceit on my part. Instead, my writing of the text strives to display a cross section of the wide range of individuals who came to live and work in places often thought by the general public to be remote, backward, or insignificant. I wanted to demonstrate that these individuals were builders of permanent residences for themselves and their families in the plains and mountains of an area that stretches from the edges of Illinois to the South Pacific and from Mexico to beyond the Arctic Circle. And, while venturing there, they made indelible impressions upon our culture, even though it has been whitewashed for the better part of three hundred years.

My interest in this endeavor derives from my background as a professor of media—especially photographic images. Therefore, this text stresses images as evidence of the existence of these individuals and not as a historical analysis of their contributions or importance. As media, photographs became part of a communications network, ultimately becoming precursors of television and motion pictures and what was to be described as "mass media." All these more modern developments massively reconstructed our understanding of American history and the contributions of ethnic groups to our development as a country.

This text focuses on approximately two hundred pictorials, ones that call unaccustomed attention to a period in North American history that has been tainted through neglect by the narrow vision of a relatively few writers—and a large number of historians. Herein are the faces and stories of some pioneers who changed the face of our continent forever.

Images

The illustrations presented in this book were taken from a wide variety of sources and formats. Although the bulk of them are photographs, many are in other forms: lithographs, line drawings, block prints, and sketches. These pictorial representations—found, as they were, in the mass media of the time—were the sole means by which the predominantly white audiences formed their ideas of not only how black men and women looked but also how they fit into the contemporary historical and political realities.

In searching for every conceivable kind of image that was to be found in newspapers, books, and periodicals, I started with the earliest to be found and stopped my search near the end of the "cattle kingdom" era in the West, circa 1910. It is this time period in which eastern readers and European audiences were learning what the greater North American West was about, who lived there, and what their roles were in the seemingly relentless westward exodus of the late nineteenth and early twentieth centuries.

These readers saw few depictions of African American men and women, even though they constituted a substantial minority of the pioneers moving west of the Mississippi and into parts of Canada and what would become the state of Alaska. We were—and probably still are—a nation that concentrated overmuch on the contributions of "majorities" in our politics and general society and downplayed that of "minorities." These attitudes are a legacy we, not suprisingly, acquired from our forebears.

Attitudes can change in the presence of new insights not previously evident. Hence, this book. The following chapters describe the range of contributions by African American pioneers who participated in North America's western expansion.

The illustrations in this book can create one sort of imagery—graphic imagery. Another sort, created through the written text, can be the pictures we form in our minds while reading about the roles of people in this country's history, and these images are indelible even if they are not "graphic." So, they, too, contribute to fresh insights.

As might be expected, the quality of hundred-year-old photographs varies widely, depending upon original sources, the skills of the photographer and the printer, as well the manner of storage. Master negatives were seldom available, except in government repositories, and often those archives possessed only copies of originals. Other than through techniques such as cleaning and rephotographing with high-quality modern film bases, few attempts were made to restore the images. Though a strong argument is possible for enhancement through digitizing or other electronic means—

indeed, this might make some pictures clearer—the majority are printed as they appear today. Only in those few cases wherein an image seemed extremely important to the text but was virtually illegible were other means used to copy the prints.

There is no attempt in this text to cover every state, territory, mountain range, or municipality in which there were black pioneers. The book would be six times its present size and unwieldy at best. Instead, my intention is to describe the little-known widespread distribution of African Americans in western areas of the continent. It will be up to other researchers to flesh out many details, and I hope additional studies will be forthcoming that will accurately examine the particulars.

1800s *Photography*

The popularity of photography in the mid- to late 1800s and early 1900s was a powerful addition to the growing acceptance of mass media as the recorders of truth. Therefore, the images that history has left us of our pioneers—of all colors—strongly influence how we view the "place" of African Americans in our country's early years.

Nearly forgotten stories of ex-slave mountain men and others of great and small achievement have been for all practical purposes lost to a large audience. However, those historical figures were some of the "images" presented to other Americans—images upon which many of the concepts of social roles, such as racial stereotyping, were based.

In their own way, all of these stereotypic images affected the cultural heritage of the Western world, not solely residents of the United States. Contained in them were standards setting forth what was respectable, acceptable, and "useful" for black men and women in our society. These concepts were, in fact, primarily limiting factors for many of the pioneers and their descendants. But, when viewed over history's shoulder, they show how many of these men and women began to break the shackles that time and society had put on them as they moved into new lands and faced new experiences.

Confusing Issues

To further complicate historical accuracy and public knowledge of the role of African Americans in western North American, what little coverage there

James Beckworth (sometimes Beckwith or Beckwourth) was a gambler, explorer, and entrepreneur who roamed the mountains and plains of Montana, Wyoming, California, Colorado, and Nevada. (Courtesy of the American Heritage Center, University of Wyoming, Laramie)

has been in the media has often been incomplete or simply wrong. For example, the African American explorer, mountain man, and a chief of the Crow Nation, James Beckworth, was once portrayed by the white actor Jack Oakie (not incidentally, a famous comedian of the times) in a motion picture.

When John Syme painted his portrait of John James Audubon in 1826, he depicted him as white. (In a European version of the same sociological issue, Camille Saint-Saëns, the French composer, who was of Haitian descent, was rarely shown in drawings. Apparently the promoters of his time thought that audiences might be repelled by his dark-skinned features.)

In total, social forces beyond those of mere historical accuracy have melded to create misleading imagery of black Americans and historical characters.

John James Audubon, as depicted in his *Birds of America*. The son of a married French sea captain and a Haitian woman, he inherited the aquiline features of his father and the skin tones—not depicted here—of his mother. (Courtesy of the White House Collection, Washington, D.C.)

Their presence in the West is not widely documented; therefore, it is not surprising that the general perception was that they were so rare as to be unimportant. It is now becoming clear that African Americans constituted approximately 1.5 to 3 percent[1] of nineteenth-century settlers in the West. Based on 1870 and 1880 population statistics, there may have been as many as 150,000 African Americans present in that part of the country. Assuming that a large percentage of these people was employed as laborers, it is likely that 15,000 to 20,000 were entrepreneurs, professionals, and leaders engaged in various endeavors in small and large communities.

1. This number is generally accepted by scholars of the American West and is reported in Wesley and Romero (1967:17).

The racism implicit in both early advertising and motion pictures is displayed in this "intermission slide" from Grand Island, Nebraska, circa 1905. Audiences were barraged with this kind of imagery. (Courtesy of the American Heritage Center, University of Wyoming, Laramie)

These are significant numbers, given the sparse settlement of the times and area. It is also clear that their influence upon those settlements and territories was far more significant than is generally credited. Clearly, then, much of what western North America has become today is derived from the cultural vitality of African American settlers.

U.S. citizens have long had problems with issues associated with skin color, ethnic groups, and slavery; it is as though our society has been simultaneously attracted to and repelled by it. For example, the statue on top of the Capitol in Washington, D.C., was originally designed by architect Thomas Crawford to be that of a man wearing a freedman's cap, the ancient Greco-Roman symbol of a slave who had been set free. This proposal was so controversial with members of Congress—strongly divided on the slavery issue—that the image was changed by Secretary of War Jefferson Davis (also in charge of construction of the Capitol and later president of the Confederacy) to the less controversial symbol of America as an allegorical young Indian woman.

At various times in history the United States has supported the concept of political and social isolationism, that is, staying away from intervention in foreign affairs. This practiced lack of interest in worldwide issues may have lent reinforcement to the idea that we reside in a unique place that is self-sufficient, self-righteous, and seemingly the sole possessor of "answers" to major world social problems with which other nations are still troubled. This simplistic self-concept seems to possess wide acceptance in contemporary society.

Our reliance on mass media, especially television and motion pictures, to spread and popularize national ideals has emphasized liberal attitudes of acceptance and tolerance while it has also categorized groups based on skin color and national origin. In those cases in which members of ethnic sub-groups have portrayed positive roles (law-enforcement officers, doctors, lawyers, etc.), they are often shown as clear exceptions to the rule and have usually served little more than to promulgate middle-class white values as if they were the answers to problems of minority groups in general. It is a confusing image that has been spread widely by mass media in the past twenty years or so.

There is, obviously, no way to change the past; the best we can often do is understand those events as well as we can in light of modern changes in knowledge and perceptions. This process depends, it seems, more on what we know about ourselves at any given time than what we know about the past. In other words: although we cannot change the historical past, the image of the past *is* constantly changing as we learn more about it.

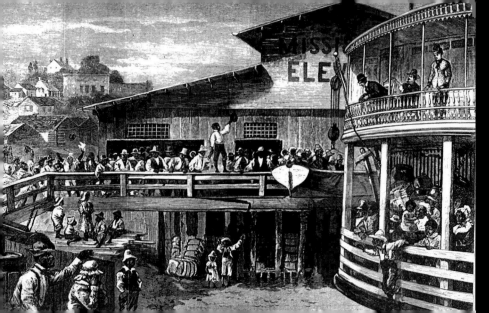

INTRODUCTION
Moving Westward and Northward

T he institution of slavery in America—while not unusual in human history—was nonetheless unique in the way it was practiced in the seventeenth through the nineteenth centuries. To begin with, never before had such large numbers of people been ripped from their homelands and transported over vast distances for delivery to a destination so alien to and so far removed from their origins. Neither had any other group been enslaved with such exclusivity to their masters with no hope of release. Even the ancient Greeks and Romans granted education and freedom as eventual rewards to their slaves.

In the American colonies and, later, the slave states and in eighteenth-century Canada, there was virtually no legal escape from bondage. In time,

(left) "Our illustration on page 284 has reference to the great movement now being made by the negro race from their accustomed homes in the South to the more tranquil region west of the Mississippi. Fugitives from injustice and oppression, these people are fleeing northward and westward, as others of their race previously fled from the horrors of slavery. Deprived of their own civil rights, they are now in their own section of our country, nearly as far from the enjoyment of the privileges granted them by the Constitution as they were in their day of bondage." (*Harper's Weekly*, May 17, 1879)

these enslaved people lost much of their individual national identity not only through systematic exclusion from their owners' society but also through permanent subjugation through the force of law.

The system, however, did not last forever. For various complex political, religious, and social reasons, institutionalized—and governmentally approved—slavery in the United States came to an end in the middle of the nineteenth century; in Canada it occurred somewhat earlier. In both countries, black citizens were given the same choices open to all free men and women to pursue their own goals in whatever ways they could. Although racial prejudice did not come to an end with Abraham Lincoln's signature on the Emancipation Proclamation or the Canadian laws outlawing slavery in the early 1800s, many of the previously existing barriers erected to stem the progress of ex-slaves were reduced if not removed entirely.

As a result, many individuals of African and West Indian descent chose to remain in the South out of familiarity or a sense of obligation, if nothing else. Oddly, some had apparently chosen to fight for the Confederacy and,

Punishing slaves as examples to others occurred with regularity and great brutality. This engraving, from England, shows a master disciplining with a cricket bat. (From author's collection)

by doing so, paid allegiance to the soil that they came to call their own.[1] Others took fate by the coattails and moved to the more industrialized North in search of better-paying jobs. A few decided to relocate to the border states, where slower life-styles blended with governments that were more accepting than the deep South. The Underground Railroad served to spirit thousands from the middle and deep South across the border into southern and western Canada and other compass points less well known.

Fewer still were pulled into the western migration that was sweeping the country at the time. Much was going on in the Old West of both the States and Canada that stretched from Kansas to California and from Alberta to New Mexico: gold in California, British Columbia, and the Yukon; cattle in Texas and the Indian territories; railroad construction by Union Pacific, Northern Pacific, Canadian Pacific, and Burlington Northern across the Great Plains; the Indian wars; bands of raiders left after the end of the Civil War. There were mountains and passes waiting to be explored and conquered by men and women courageous or foolhardy enough to try. At sea, there were fisheries in the Sandwich Islands and northern Pacific and Atlantic Oceans. Opportunities for those with able bodies and minds seemed to abound, and thousands of former slaves decided to try for their shares of the American dream.

Essentially, the migratory patterns of African Americans from the Old South followed the railways that were gradually connecting heretofore isolated areas; many railways followed original American Indians' trails. Some of the earliest job opportunities available to these new emigrants were on the trains as porters, butchers, waiters, cooks, service personnel, loaders, and baggage clerks—about any job except those already taken by the European immigrants who had arrived earlier and had the "front end" occupations of engineers, firemen, and station clerks.

Ultimately, the job of conductor became almost the sole domain of a

---

1. Researchers into the history of African Americans who are U.S. citizens eventually stumble across vague references to black men who fought on the side of the Confederacy. Although assiduous scholars have searched diligently for the evidence, not one has found a "mustering out" list of any "Negro" soldiers from southern regiments. Still, the stories persist. The stories most likely grew out of the action of the Virginia legislature in 1865, which tried to establish two black state units. The Civil War ended prior to the enactment of the bill. If, however, records of these soldiers were to be found, it would be solid evidence of how deeply the system of slavery became ingrained in those on both sides of the practice—creating some previously enslaved individuals so accommodated to the system that they thought it worthy of defense. Maybe no one will ever know the truth.

Conductors and loaders on the Northern Pacific Railroad, circa 1890. To most railway travelers of the era, service jobs like these were the only ones they associated with African Americans. (From author's collection)

black man if he stayed at it long enough. Still, there were other jobs to be had and men and women willing to take them, whatever they were.

Many of these job hunters stopped and stayed along the train routes, creating niches in the growing economies of the small towns that sprang up to meet the demands of the railroads. By 1900, for instance, the overwhelming majority of barbers in the country were African American—a fact often overlooked by historians and authors in general.

The way west for these newly relocated citizens was inextricably mixed with the movement of others also searching for personal success and unique challenges. Immigrant Irish, Chinese, English, Scottish, Scandinavian, German, and Russian workers were just beginning an influx that would peak within fifty years. Also in the mix were French Canadians who could trace their fur-trapping ancestors back into the 1700s.

As opportunities for employment began to stratify, entrepreneurs and hustlers dominated the economic life of the new cities and towns; unskilled laborers were forced to gravitate toward labor-intensive positions like working cattle or heavy industrial jobs; women were less likely to find employment as a result of social stereotyping, and they were primarily untrained workers to begin with. Blacks, Chinese, Japanese, Indians, and individuals of "mixed blood" were at the bottom of the job ladder, having to take whatever was left over.

Or so it seemed to historians of the early twentieth century as they looked back on those times. As with all such generalizations, there were many and varied exceptions—for example, the actual roles played by African Americans. Late in the twentieth century, we are only beginning to realize the full range of activities in which the pioneers of the vast two-thirds of our continent engaged. Heretofore, prejudices, myopia, cultural insensitivity, invalid surveys—call them what you will—have dominated much of the examination of this period of American history. We have often seen what we wanted to see rather than what was there. The popular media of the time—as well as a pervasive longing for a sense of identity—compounded the problem by producing stories about heroes who either never existed or were dramatically modified to appeal to the sentiments of mainly white readers of newspapers, buyers of penny-dreadfuls, motion picture audiences, and—much later—television viewers.

Auction of slaves in Texas, lithograph, circa 1860. Although there were images of individuals in servile occupations, more drawings of them as slaves at auction appeared in the media of the times. (Courtesy of the Institute for Texan Cultures, San Antonio)

"The Boy Pard of Texas Jack," in 1887, one of the few images of a penny-dreadful's black hero to survive from the past. Although he was the "sidekick" of the protagonist, he did gain top billing on the cover. (From author's collection)

As perspectives became distorted, it was nearly impossible to separate fact from fiction. Minorities became less and less important in history texts, popular entertainments, and casual conversations. Nonwhites ceased to exist, essentially, in these aspects of our nation's history. Slavery, to book and penny-dreadful readers (and television and film viewers of the twentieth century), became little more than a dramatic device—a piece of theater that white readers barely could imagine let alone experience.

In all fairness, this erasure of nonanglos from our background as a nation was probably not done solely through malevolence; it may not have been simple oversight either. Rather, it seems that much of the history of this continent involved "superior" invading forces from foreign cultures taking life and property from those who were already living here. In order to avoid a depressing self-concept, the dominant, white society has systematically sought to justify these acts of aggression. After all, it does not fit well with the "American ideal" to think that theft, rape, and—at times—wanton destruction were the principal means by which we grew and prospered as a nation. There must be—the explanation goes—a better rationale behind all of this evil-doing to justify the success of our social, technological, and economic experiment.

This self-defensive attitude of Manifest Destiny has a calming effect for many. For example, it encourages the acceptance of the inevitability of one society's domination by another as "growth" or "natural law." This rationale is far more pleasing to some than the alternatives: that one group was merely stronger, more technically advanced, or richer than those it came to dominate.

So, by design or omission, plan or default, our cultural heritage has been rewritten to conform to what we think is true rather than to what actually happened. It is not the first time (nor the first society) in which words have been used in an attempt to alter facts, but the result has been a particularly effective restructuring of facts.

In actuality, African Americans played the same roles in the development of western North America as did other ethnic groups. They fought and died, raised children, killed and were killed, smuggled, lied, whored; they were God-loving and God-fearing, lawmen and outlaws, mountaineers and townspeople; millionaires and paupers; they built cities and towns and destroyed them, too; they danced, cried, fought Indians, protected travelers, and so forth.

"Colored" men and women were assigned, in the spirit of the times, to relatively insignificant places in society, since their numbers made it impossible for them to be ignored totally. Menial occupations became jobs they could hold without offending the more numerous nonblacks who populated cities and towns. In this environment, human individuality mutated into stereotypic "facts," as servants, laborers, dissemblers, and shufflers were invariably interpreted in novels, textbooks, stories, and films of African descendants. "It's in their blood," the saying went.

In fact, former slaves and their progeny were spending their days and nights much the same as their fair-skinned compatriots of the time. For every white con man, there was a black one; for every asian laundryman, there was a black one—or a white one, for that matter. Life was as complex

Advertising cards from the 1880s. Often differing racial stereotypes were inserted with identical advertising copy on each. The chief effect, clearly, was to reinforce popular beliefs about a person's appearance and social worth. (From author's collection)

for people then as it is now, and those who experienced it were just as hard-pressed to exist and grow as are many today.

"The West"

We, who profess to be christians, and boast of the peculiar advantages we enjoy by means of an express revelation of our duty from heaven, are in effect these very untaught and heathen countries. With all our superior light, we instill into those, whom we call savage and barbarous, the most despicable opinion of human nature. We, to the utmost of our power, weaken and dissolve the universal tie, that binds and unites mankind. . . . Good God! may the time come when thou shalt stretch out thy strong arm, and say to his mighty deluge, which is sweeping myriads and myriads to enthraldom and a degraded servitude, who are entitled to equal rights and privileges with ourselves, hitherto shalt thou come, and no further, and here shall thou proud waves be stayed!

(From Ogden 1905)

North America was, in many ways, segmented in its attractiveness to emigrants, especially those recently freed from slavery. The trans-Mississippi West became a lure to some who sought to leave the Old South and find

Cowboys in Bonham, Texas, circa 1900. Such men and boys constituted large numbers of trail hands during the "cattle kingdom" years and beyond. (Courtesy of the Amon Carter Museum, Fort Worth, Texas)

success and prosperity, and their presence in northern and eastern parts of the United States and Canada dates from the seventeenth and eighteenth centuries. Farms and plantations of the South and the domestic quarters of French Canada ("New France") became the main residences of former slaves, and their presence was part of the social and political realities over more than two centuries.

Riding along on the migratory routes were the stereotypes and myths that seem to accompany all newcomers into areas populated with large numbers of earlier settlers. If the South had myths based on appearance, religion, skin color, and educational levels, so did the West.

In colonial times, for example, areas west of New York and Philadelphia were "terra incognita," and Canada was a haven for traitors, rascals, Royalists, and runaways, as far as many residents of the States were concerned.

By the nineteenth century, Ohio, Indiana, and Tennessee were the outermost reaches of U.S. expansion. By mid-century, large-scale migration west and north, across the Great Plains, had changed the lines once again.

The trans-Mississippi West became a relatively concise designation for "the West" when the U.S. military fort system began in earnest with the construction of Fort Atkinson to protect river traffic on the Missouri in 1819. Consistent with the military's mission to protect travelers, barges, and small communities, the fort system was expanded when Congress authorized construction of railroads across the Plains. Fort Laramie and Fort Hall, plus other installations in the Southwest, were established to control the American Indians who were resisting incursions into and through their historical lands. Additionally, these outposts protected wagon trains heading toward the west coast as well as an enlarged web of railroads that would serve the growing cattle empires of the West and Southwest.

Eventually, U.S. forts and the military would become centers for new communities when some travelers tarried and a few enlisted mens' families did not return to their homes back East.

As a result, the West as a concept came to typify the last frontier of the United States' part of the continent. In the process, it became not only a place but also a mystic, marvelous, mythological part of the American psyche, which was celebrated in song, dance, story, and film. It became a cultural identifier uniquely dissimilar to the urbanity of New York City, the industrial dynamism of Chicago, or the agricultural fiefdoms of pre–Civil War Georgia.

The West became a unique, if generalized, part of this continent's history and culture. It became the place from which, according to observers like historian Frederick Jackson Turner, we sprang as a nation: a strong, open, wonder-filled place that permeates our modern life and stimulates our self-concepts, industry, and even religions. In our popular mythology, it was populated with characters of strength, durability, and purpose—and they were almost all white.

It wasn't like that at all—hence, the reason for this book. Instead of settling for "myth," we need to know the facts of our past. Reality, truth, and historical perspective are more important and revealing than fiction— no matter how dramatically structured—in helping us assess the past, and they may help us to understand who we are, where we came from, and— most important—where we are going.

The Western Period

The West, at bottom, is a form of society, rather than an area. It is the term applied to the region whose social conditions result from the application of older institutions and ideas to the transforming influences of free land.

(From Turner 1929:278)

What is "the West," anyway? Tangled up in our cultural myths about pioneers, wagon trains, Indian skirmishes, cavalry outposts, land-grabbers, gold rushes, vast spaces, gunfighters, and bad men (and women) are the realities of life in those times and places.

James Beckworth

Not many black men rose to the level of "legendary" in the American West, but Dark Sky (James Beckworth's Sac Indian name) was an exception. In fact, Beckworth's life was exceptional in so many ways as to truly earn the appellation "heroic."

A freed slave and the son of a white, transplanted St. Louis blacksmith, "Sir Jennings Beckwoth" (note the variant spelling) spent his first years in the fur-trading era of the early 1800s watching and listening to the tall tales of those mainly French-Canadian explorers who came down the Missouri and Mississippi Rivers for trade, recreation, and human contact. In 1824 he asked his father[2] what he should do with his life, and was told to follow

2. James Beckworth's slave master was also his father. The resulting light skin was possibly one reason he was readily accepted into the business of trading.

BLACK PIONEERS

his yearnings. Later that year he signed on with William H. Ashley's expedition out of St. Louis as a wrangler and body servant. It was only a short association since, within a year, he was an independent trapper buying "mounts" (an old term for furs) from the Pawnees. His lot was cast forever.

Beckworth ventured westward in search of the mountains, sharing the vast areas of the Great Plains and Northwest with white mountain men like Jim Bridger, Kit Carson, and Jedediah Smith. He also roamed throughout the Southwest, the Cascades, and the Dacotah Territory fighting Indians, Mexicans, and the weather. He was not the only African American to take up this solitary trade: Edward Rose and Dred Scott—whose slavery indenture was upheld by the U.S. Supreme Court in later years—also sought their fortunes in the high mountains.

Beckworth's achievements in the wilds of the West culminated in his becoming "chief of chiefs" of the Crow Indian nation in 1834 for seven years—an almost unheard of honor for any non-Indian. He married "Sue," a Santee woman; "discovered" the pass in northern California/Nevada that bears his name; and pioneered the Oregon Trail through Crow country. In later years, he opened a bar and other businesses in a small village on Cherry Creek that would become Denver, Colorado.

His exploits are recorded in his autobiography, which blends factual stories of his adventures with the garrulous and often outrageous tales that mountain men perfected into an art form.

(left) Frontispiece from *The Autobiography of James Beckworth.* Note the anglicized features when compared to the photograph in the Preface. (From author's collection)

CHAPTER TWO

The Society of Friends [Quakers] were the first, I believe, in America, who publicly denounced slavery as incompatible with the christian religion; and slave holders as unqualified to become worthy members of their truly religious society.

(Ogden 1905)

EARLY IMAGERY

In the early years of the nineteenth century, newspapers and magazines were virtually the only popular forms of what would be later called "mass media." These publications were central to the spreading of information about westward expansion, politics, or local and world events. They also had a more widespread circulation than they do today as well as more influence on their readers, most of whom regarded them highly and believed their editors to be trustworthy. The public regarded these periodicals as unimpeachable sources of information about world events and believed that editors allowed only "important issues" to be covered.

(left) This image, drawn from life by an artist for *Harper's Weekly* in the 1860s, is an early one published by the media. It depicts a group of Shakers dancing, with what is probably a runaway slave (figure on extreme right) joining in. The Shakers were noted for assisting runaways who were traveling north on the Underground Railroad. (From author's collection)

The job of photographer on the American and Canadian frontiers was a far more demanding, lonely, and risky affair than a comparable assignment is today. Cameras and developing equipment were not only large and clumsy but also fragile and expensive to maintain. The person who set out to make a living through portrait photography in small, out-of-the-way settlements faced great physical and financial challenges. If an income were to be made, much of it would have to come from the small charges assessed for informal—or non-"studio"—images rather than the occasional photograph of a wealthy or famous individual.

Eventually recognized as an inexpensive substitute for the costly oil portrait, photography became the means by which an individual of moderate means could achieve a degree of immortality similar to that available to the affluent. Consequently, a traveling photographer not only earned an income but also became a figure in the popular mythology of the times as "an artist."

It is difficult to imagine how those "artists," who drove wagons loaded with cameras, film, glass plates, caustic chemicals, and repair supplies, managed on a day-to-day basis. Yet, they seem to have covered the West, Canada, and frozen regions of Alaska with alacrity and efficiency. Their work exists in thousands of images, which have survived even after the passing of a century, and it is in these more casual photographs that much about everyday life of those times can be assessed—life that included the mundane as well as the magnificent.

Typically, an itinerant photographer—only men are known from this early period—would enter a town with little advance notice. If there was a newspaper, he might take out a small advertisement to announce his arrival. More likely, however, he would rely on simple word of mouth, or he might perform some services gratis to gain attention.

Apparently, one of the most common techniques used by these early entrepreneurs on arrival was to pay a visit to the local saloon. He knew that there would be a ready assembly of potential customers in the bar and that every customer with a family would probably want the ubiquitous "family portrait," which could be had for a relatively small sum.

By offering the men a chance to have their pictures taken—ordinarily outdoors, "hanging out" in front of the bar or hotel where the sun was bright and the camera setup was quick and easy—the photographer recorded not only scenes of everyday happenings but also inadvertent evidence of African American men, women, and children as part of the cultural life.

As this collection of images shows, life on the streets of western settle-

Chinese workers arrived in America to help build railroads, establish businesses, and work in the mines of the West. Their presence—like that of African Americans—was not always appreciated or tolerated. Captioned "Massacre of Chinese at Rock Springs, Wyoming—Drawn by T. de Thulstrup from photographs by Lieutenant C. A. Booth, Seventh United States Infantry" (*Harper's Weekly*, September 26, 1885), the scene depicts a white miners' revolt against the hiring of Chinese to work in the coal mines. The result was several hundred dead Asians, most killed by bombs placed in the mine shafts while they worked. (From author's collection)

ments was a far greater amalgam of differing social and ethnic groups than many of these same towns display in the late twentieth century.

Beginning in the late 1700s, publications employed itinerant sketch artists, painters, and lithographers to add visual variety to solid pages of newsprint. Artists like Frederick Remington earned substantial incomes and became known for their drawings. Nineteenth-century popular publications—those with a large circulation—put lithographs on the front page of nearly every issue. Later, they would dedicate even more space to pictures of contemporary events. As with readers today, visual images caught the attention of customers as they passed newsstands; and what the customers apparently were interested in buying, editors were more than willing to print more of.

Some publications became nothing more than page after page of pictures with little or no written commentary. By the latter part of the century, rotogravure sections with no captions became commonplace in publications in large North American cities. Clearly, the age of photojournalism had begun.

The lithograph became a means of capturing a moment in time, of providing visual comprehension of events and participants as well as adding excitement to news copy. A picture became "worth ten thousand words." Increasingly, words became mere locators and identifiers of content, clearly secondary to the images. Readers became "viewers," finding the pictures to be not only attractive elements of the periodicals but also self-evident and self-contained news "items." Pictures provided "truth," "accuracy," and "believability."

Pictures at War

Photojournalism played an important role in one of America's most dramatic historical events: the Civil War. It is often argued that the Civil War was the first "popular war" in U.S. history, since neither the Revolutionary War nor various regional conflicts that occurred during the early years of the Republic had the support of a majority of the citizenry. Also, reporting of events was very limited due to the small size of the colonial press. The Civil War involved all then-existing states and territories, whose citizens, respectively, were either States' Righters or Unionists—and fence-sitters were essentially nonexistent.

(*top right*) "Come and Join Us, Brothers," one of the most well-known recruiting posters of the Civil War, successfully encouraged young black men to join the Union forces. (Courtesy of the National Archives, Washington, D.C.)

(*bottom right*) Black soldiers stand guard outside a southern business taken in a military siege. (Matthew Brady photograph, courtesy of the National Archives, Washington, D.C.)

COME AND JOIN US BROTHERS.

Newspapers and magazines from the North, South, and West sent correspondents, sketch artists, and a few photographers to the battlefields to cover the engagements. Those few photographers were to become as much a part of history as the war was. It was the first armed conflict to be covered by photographers in the field, and Matthew Brady was to become famous for his images of the drama and horror of the war. His photographs were at least as articulate in reporting events as any written description or analysis.

The Photographs

Locating nineteenth-century photographs of African Americans in the West, Canada, and Alaska is a difficult assignment at best. The search is complicated by the fact that photography became popular only after the Civil War, and even then was the domain of professionals who used studios for their posed creations. It was only after George Eastman introduced photographic equipment like the hand-held Kodak folding camera late in the century that informal "snapshots" taken by ordinary citizens became popular.

As a result, the earliest known photographs were usually made by professionals: tintypes, daguerreotypes, ambrotypes, glass-plate negatives and glass slide positives, *cartes de visite* (CDV's), cabinet photographs, and numerous other types. Since few bore any identifying information, a degree of detective work was necessary to date them and determine their points of origin. Sometimes only the most general identifiers were possible, such as "California area" or "northern Plains territories," for example.

Provenance was another troubling issue. Although some photographs have information about the subjects and locales written on the back, most do not. Reasonable speculation about the subjects, their occupations, and social status had to be deduced from clues such as background details, type of photograph, location, and so forth. Because of their rarity it is not surprising that few particulars are available for many of them. Until further research unearths more relevant material, the description of many photographs will remain incomplete.

What is "of African Descent?"

A multiplicity of issues surrounds the use of the word "race." In the late twentieth century, anthropologists and sociologists are calling its definition more and more into question.[1] Initially used as a method of sorting human beings into subgroups by means of observed, external physical differences, the terminology begins to fall apart in light of DNA studies. There are no "racial" DNA's. The concept of race in describing human differences is no longer scientifically valid.

Beyond skin color, a person's racial heritage and proof thereof can assume social, political, geographic, religious, and cultural importance. A person's search for his or her roots—an ancestral source—begins with whatever racial and cultural heritage is relevant. The search for pictorial images of black pioneers likewise involved recognizing which ones were relevant and which were not. While it may seem obvious that one image appears to be that of a black person and another is not, it is not that simple.

A quick review of census records from the nineteenth century reveals that the census takers were not always explicit or precise in their written commentaries—more likely, the inconsistencies were inevitable. Their use of such terms as "Negro," "African," "mulatto," "half-breed," "octoroon," and others are confusing and inexact. Quite often these records reflect the census-takers' highly personal impressions of race or ethnicity. Other times, the individuals questioned had provided the information.

Not surprisingly, there was no consensus on the meanings of the terms. For example, in some western locations, "mulatto" might mean "half black, half white" or "half Indian, half black" or "half white, half Indian." Similarly, dark-skinned "negritos" and "meztisos" from Mexico might be listed as "Indian."

Since my original intention for this book was to include a wide variety of pictorial images rather than miss any that might be important, I did not base my selections on the terms used by the census takers. Those images of individuals who identified themselves as "black" were accepted at face value and are included. A statement by a contemporary who seemed to have no ulterior motive in describing another as "Negro" also validated the image for inclusion. For those images lacking provenances, selection was difficult, so they must stand on their merits alone.

From times preceding slavery until the present, people with different racial heritages have married and had children, some of which have identified themselves with a single racial group or more. Some have "passed"

1. In the summer of 1995, the American Anthropological Association passed a resolution stating that "differentiating species into biologically defined 'races' has proven meaningless and unscientific. . . ." Although there may be political or social evidence for this concept, science cannot support such distinctions (American Anthropological Association, *Newsletter* 36[1]:3).

Young Bat and Mrs. Slaughter relaxing inside a shed, circa 1885. Individuals of many racial heritages and cultures existed side by side in a time not generally remembered for interracial socializing. (Courtesy of the John Slaughter State Park, Arizona)

and have identified themselves with a racial group by choice rather than by biological background. The possible combinations are too numerous as well as lacking significance for consideration here.

So, for better or for worse, included are images of individuals who are identified as being black, who appear to be black, or were attested to by family and friends as being black. I accept any criticism that might derive from this decision. It seems far more important to show the widespread presence of African American pioneers in the North American continent than to err in favor of a policy so restrictive that the issue is clouded and reduced in importance.

"Hanging out" in front of the Antwerp Saloon, Portland, Oregon, circa 1888. The Antwerp was a meeting place, primarily, for members of the Belgian community in Portland, but obviously not limited to their patronage. (Courtesy of the Oregon Historical Society, Portland)

CHAPTER THREE

BLACK WESTERNERS IN
WHITE MYTHOLOGY

I n the nineteenth century, newspaper reporters and sketch artists traveled with migrating throngs, sending back words about and visual
images of the newest pioneers in the West. These reporters used fact
and fiction to create a population of white sheriffs, city builders, and entrepreneurs with which their primarily eastern readers could identify, thereby
giving birth to most of the myths about the West. Add to this illusion the
growing popularity in the East of western novels by such authors as Zane
Grey and Owen Wister, and a distorted picture of western pioneers began
to emerge. Later, magazines, comic books, radio programs, motion pictures, and television would compound this more than somewhat erroneous rendition of western pioneers.

Seldom covered were the roles played by African American men and
women as explorers, expedition guides, managers, and workers on ranches.

(*left*) Master Carter Jackson posed, bandaged fingers and all, before the camera
circa 1900 in Green River, Wyoming. This style of studio portrait, which was
neither rare nor inexpensive, helped change stereotypes of African Americans'
outward appearance in the white media of the times. (Courtesy of the Wyoming
State Museum and Archive, Cheyenne)

Women washing clothes for the military during the Civil War. Such images strengthened stereotypic impressions of African Americans. (*Harper's Weekly,* January 16, 1864; from author's collection)

Although the Lewis and Clark expedition and the Hayden mapping expedition into the Northwest Territories employed African American men in important positions, it was not until the twentieth century that these facts were revealed. Little or none of this information was ever published in the nineteenth century.

Readers of newspapers, magazines, and other print media could acquire an intellectual understanding of the place of minorities in America's westward expansion; but, with the addition of graphic art to the various media, subscribers acquired an enhanced, or "popular," image of the West and its inhabitants. This response by eastern readers contributed to the core of erroneous but widespread perceptions of the social roles of American Indians, Asians, Mexicans/Hispanics, and blacks in western history.

Written and pictorial representations in popular publications as well as in stereographs and advertisements were responsible for what would become accepted as "common knowledge" about minorities in the United States. These misconceptions have existed in one form or another for the past 150 years.

The First Images

The first pictorial representations of African Americans published for predominantly white audiences were those of slavery. The most popular periodicals of the time—*Harper's Weekly, Canadian Illustrated,* and *Leslie's Illustrated Weekly,* for example—published millions of lithographic engravings (the first "photographs") of African Americans in a variety of stereotypic situations. The contents of these publications were granted a high credibility by their readers, to whom words and especially pictures were accepted as true and enlightening. The words and pictures validated the prevailing attitudes of most whites toward black individuals as accurate.

Many advertisements of the time were scurrilously racist, portraying African Americans as unable to speak well, reason intelligently, or conduct themselves with socially acceptable manners or mores.

Most of the printed images in circulation for predominantly white consumers were singularly racist portrayals of African Americans. Clearly, these images not only affected white conceptions of "appropriate" roles for African Americans in society but also tainted the treatment that they received

Depictions of slaves being bought and sold, such as this frame of a stereograph from the 1860s, were commonplace, reinforcing the view that they were nothing more than possessions. (From author's collection)

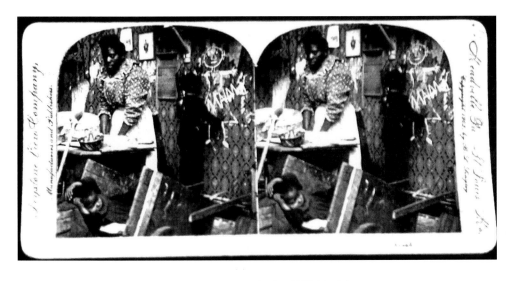

(top) Highly popular throughout the country, stereographs from the late 1800s usually portrayed black individuals as household servants, menial laborers, chicken thieves, wastrels, and other demeaning characterizations. These images were often the only ones many whites saw of African Americans. (Keystone View Co., 1902 stereograph; author's collection)

An Arbuckle coffee card, circa 1890. These pocket-sized cards were used by traveling salesmen as a "humourous" gimmick to attract buyers and with whom they could share a laugh or two. Given the times, such cards were not seen as racist, as they would be judged today. The coffee prices were listed on the reverse side of the card. (From author's collection)

Barbering was essentially a "black" occupation in the United States prior to
1900, as this image from Ann Arbor, Michigan, illustrates. Only after the turn of
the century did it become "white." (From author's collection)

in textbooks, classrooms, and living rooms across the country—to say nothing of their treatment in seeking employment and by social institutions as
they moved out of slavery.

As mentioned in the Introduction, when freed slaves began to look for
jobs, only the lowermost rungs on economic ladders were available to
them; and these were usually already filled by European immigrants, most
of whom were white. Consequently, only menial occupations were left.[1] In
the West, for example, the most desirable and well-paid jobs with railroads
and mining companies were quickly filled primarily by Irish, English, German, and Scandinavian immigrants. The leftovers were taken by African
Americans and Hispanics. Thus, photographs of the time were of these
workers in menial jobs; another kind of image did not exist to be recorded.

1. Forty-one black barbers were listed in Des Moines, Iowa, in 1895. The number was so
large that Bergmann (1969:47) explained that it was normal and acceptable for white patrons
to visit these parlors in the West.

In the mid-South, along the Mississippi River, black men and women also took what they could find: work on riverboat crews and as waiters and fruit pickers.

Western Roles

Itinerant photographers of the late 1800s enjoyed much the same stature as the lithographers and sketch artists who had preceded them. In the West, they found a ready audience for their photographic skills with their glass plates and sensitized sheets of copper to capture images of people in formal and everyday poses. Although most of the subjects were white, many were not.

The U.S. military provided many opportunities for African Americans to participate in western pageantry. Despite Hollywood's versions, it was buffalo soldiers who were assigned to protect most of the pioneer wagon trains venturing west. Although most of the travelers were white, some were black, but their exploits are virtually unrecorded.

Competition for work—or for any advantageous position—led to innumerable conflicts based on racial prejudice between African Americans and the white culture around them. Typically—and regretfully—lynchings were an all too common a method of resolving problems raised by interracial conflict. Any individual, regardless of ethnic background, was "brought to justice" if believed guilty of a perceived violation of the western code. Not surprising, lynchings occupied a special niche in the history of the mythical West.

The westward movement brought murder, injustice, and violence with

(top left) River flatboat used on the shallow rivers of the West for ferrying materials and travelers. (Courtesy of the Montana State Historical Society, Helena)

(top right) Photography was among the many technological developments of the nineteenth century. A few black entrepreneurs entered this business, as did W. L. Goodridge of Saginaw, Michigan, circa 1900. He is probably the man shown leaning in the doorway. (From author's collection)

(bottom) "Hanging out" at a saloon in North Dakota, circa 1890. This photograph illustrates the inclusion of African Americans in the everyday activities of western life. (Courtesy of the North Dakota State Historical Society, Bismarck)

Wagon train near Saratoga, Wyoming, circa 1890. Unlike the well-provisioned groups of whites, African Americans often trekked westward with minimal supplies and few guides, following in the wagon tracks of others. (Courtesy of Dick Perue Historical Photos, Saratoga, Wyoming)

it; and a substantial portion of the lawlessness was caused by racial prejudice and an insensitivity regarding human life. All was not death and destruction, however. Many African Americans, like Barney Ford, saw opportunities in the businesses springing up in the new cities and towns of the West. They became the entrepreneurs who established hotels, schools, newspapers, and other enterprises that served everyone. Similarly, in Trinidad,

(top right) A lynching in Green River, Wyoming, 1895. Sometimes validated by quasi-judicial proceedings, lynching was the most common penalty in dealing with perceived or real miscreants of all ethnic backgrounds in the early West. (Courtesy of the Wyoming State Museum and Archive, Cheyenne)

(bottom right) Unfortunately, lynchings were a part of "normal" western existence. A town too small to support an adequate police force relied on a local *posses comitatus* to mete out punishments. Some lynchings, however, were carried out by an angry and dangerous mob without legal authority. This 1904 event, in Laramie, Wyoming, resulted from an aborted jailbreak and vicious attack on a white woman by Joe Martin, a black prisoner. He was summarily hanged by a local mob. (Courtesy of the American Heritage Center, University of Wyoming, Laramie)

Drawing from Associated Press Release.

XI. One More Lynching In Laramie

There was the time after the turn of the century when the townsmen used the rope again.

Confined in the county jail in August, 1904, was "a human degenerate Joe Martin, negro" using the name of Joe Smith. He had just served three years in the Wyoming penitentiary (now relocated at Rawlins) for a bestial crime.

Judge Carpenter had sentenced him to six months in the local jail for sending obscene letters through the mail. On this particular day he was caught in a lynching web of his own brutal instincts.

The wife of Sheriff Alfred Cook had engaged a sixteen-year-old girl, Della Krause to assist her in the courthouse kitchen. Della was peeling potatoes when she heard a loud scuffling noise behind her. Turning she saw Joe Martin coming at her. The prisoner had managed to spring the lock of his cell by prying it with the steel coil from the springs of his cot. He had in the same manner been able to open a cupboard of general use in which was kept shaving items. He had grabbed a razor and now came slashing at Miss Krause.

The sheriff's wife hearing the screams rushed to the scene just as the girl with her throat gashed open slipped to the floor. Mrs. Cook grabbed the negro's arms and was able by sheer strength to pinion him, all the while yelling for help.

Sheriff Cook and a deputy came running and the captive was beaten into submission and cast back into his cell, but not before he had with suicidal intentions haggled his own throat and was wallowing in his own blood.

Dr. Stevens was summoned and pronounced Della would live, but would be disfigured for life. The Boomerang put out a special edition of the fiendish attack, and all afternoon men huddled together on a street

Barney Ford, hotelkeeper, entrepreneur, gold miner in Nicaragua, civic leader in Wyoming and Colorado, who also served as a member of the statehood committees for both states. (Courtesy of the Wyoming State Museum and Archive, Cheyenne)

Colorado, in the 1880s, a sizeable number of African American men and women established themselves as professionals. Nancy Phillips is one such example. A nurse and midwife, she served all ethnic groups.

Black Cowboys

Historians estimate that between three and nine thousand black cowboys[2] worked on just one of the western cattle trails, the Goodnight-Loving "Long Trail" (from west Texas to Montana Territory), during the great days of the "cattle kingdom," circa 1860 to 1910.[3] When the tallies of African American men who worked on the other trails that crisscrossed the

---

2. The term "cowboy" did not have as widespread a use as is assumed today. "Cowpoke," "cowhand," and "brushpopper" (for young wranglers of stock) were the terms perferred by the men doing the work.

3. The number of men in the cowboying trade is difficult to assess, but records support a *minimal* number of 40,000 total employment, with 25 to 30 percent African Americans, Hispanics, and American Indians (Jordan n.d.:165).

(top) Job opportunities kept pace with the growing businesses in western towns. In Texas, for example, these men found work as draymen. (Courtesy of the Collins Street Bakery, Corsicana, Texas)

(bottom) "Aunt" Nancy Phillips, nurse and midwife in remote Wyoming gold-strike towns, became a beloved resident of Rock Springs and Green River near the turn of the century. (Courtesy of the Sweetwater County Library, Green River, Wyoming)

Like thousands of others throughout the West, these black cowboys worked over a period of many years on the A. E. Gillespie Ranch, in southern Wyoming. (Courtesy of W. Gordon Gillespie, Laramie, Wyoming)

western territories are considered, no fewer than ten thousand of them must have "punched cattle" in the West.

Black ranch hands performed the same duties as white ones, and were often given important responsibilities such as ramrods (ranch foremen), cooks, and horsebreakers.

Just as there were white badmen on the western scene, there were also black badmen who played their roles with the same kind of of dedication. One of the "Black Barts" of the Dakota Territory was an African American (Black Bart was an infamous white outlaw of the time). Others, like Isom Dart, robbed and plundered their way into American history. Stories of their deeds merged with those of their white contemporaries, becoming part of western legend and lore.

Isom Dart, bandit and rancher, lived and worked in the Colorado/Utah/
Wyoming area in the late 1880s. Some apocrypha claim he was shot and killed by
the notorious Butch Cassidy near Brown's Hole in northwestern Colorado. Yet
another story places his demise near Wolcott, Wyoming, after a failed bank
robbery. (Courtesy of the Savery Museum, Savery, Wyoming)

CHAPTER FOUR

WARRIORS AND SOLDIERS

The military forces have long been sources of employment for young men and women; historically, they have been places where African American men, for example, could find salaried occupations, career advancement, and camaraderie as well as a place to retreat from social and familial pressures. For whatever reasons, they have joined the military since the Revolutionary War in relatively large numbers.

The Buffalo Soldiers

In the Civil War, over 175,00 African American men fought in the Union army in the Negro Volunteer Corps. When the conflict was over, black troopers were assigned to the western frontier, where they had problems

(left) Edwin Byron Atwood, Sergeant Major of the Forty-First Ohio Infantry, fought in the battles of Murfeesboro, Tennessee; Chickamauga, Georgia; and Mission Ridge, Tennessee. Here he poses for his mustering-out photo. (From author's collection)

(top) The Tenth Cavalry on bivouac, near Chloride, Colorado, in 1885 or 1890. (Courtesy of the Museum of New Mexico, Santa Fe)

(bottom) Troopers of the Tenth Cavalry stationed at Fort Randall, Dakota Territory, circa 1880, with their requisite white officers. (Courtesy of the Library of Congress, Washington, D.C.)

Many African American troopers—like these of the Tenth Cavalry from Fort Huachuca, Arizona, depicted by Frederick Remington (second from right, his three-hundred-pound girth reduced by artistic license)—stayed on in the West, forming a corps of trained horsemen that joined the expanding "cattle kingdom" that lasted until the 1920s. (Courtesy of the American Heritage Center, University of Wyoming, Laramie)

with Mexicans and engaged in the Indian Wars for approximately forty years. There were more than 10,000 who fought in the infantry and cavalry, all in segregated units under the command of white officers.[1]

Based in the Plains and the Southwest, these enlisted men fought the Sioux, Apache, Comanche, Cheyenne, and other Indian "belligerents"; protected the southern border with Mexico; and guarded pioneer wagon trains.

As mentioned previously, the U.S. Military Fort System was established to protect migration routes in support of western expansion by fighting

1. John J. Pershing was given the nickname "Black Jack" after his assignment to the Tenth Cavalry in Arizona as a young man. Later, when he attended West Point, his fellow cadets used the term in derision. At first, Pershing was irritated by the sobriquet. Later, however, he seemed to warm to the title and its inferences, becoming proud of the bravery and loyalty of the black troops he commanded on incursions against Pancho Villa. He used the nickname for the rest of his life.

The Tenth Cavalry football team at Fort Robinson, Nebraska, home of "buffalo soldiers" for nearly forty years. (Courtesy of the Nebraska State Historical Society, Lincoln)

the American Indians who resented and resisted the influx of white settlers, traders, entrepreneurs—and the military itself. The Ninth and Tenth Cavalries were regularly rotated through almost all of the western forts, with especially long stays at Fort Robinson, Nebraska; Fort Sill, Oklahoma; Fort Huachuca, Arizona; Fort Jefferson Davis, Texas; and Fort D.A. Russell in Wyoming.[2] (All of these forts are preserved in whole or in part and stand today as mute monuments to the black experience in the U.S. military.)

Immediately following the Civil War, the U.S. War Department formed four Negro divisions to serve, primarily, in the Southwest. (Originally, the Thirty-Eighth through the Forty-First Infantries were designated "colored." Within a matter of months they were regrouped into the Twenty-Fourth and Twenty-Fifth Infantries and the Ninth and Tenth Cavalries.) These units were initially staffed with new recruits and soldiers who had served in the war and who wanted to continue their military careers. At that time, commanders in Washington, D.C., believed that black soldiers, although

2. This Wyoming fort was the only military installation to house—at different times—all four black military divisions. At one time, three were in residence simultaneously.

A rare close-up of a black soldier wearing an authentic buffalo-hide coat. (Courtesy of the Coe Library, Reference Section, University of Wyoming, Laramie)

"good and true warriors," should be limited because of their "heritage and inclination" solely to assignments *below* the fortieth parallel. The commanders believed that men of African descent could not tolerate cold, northern temperatures. This racist canard (similar to relegating black soldiers to "kitchen duty and the valet service" in World War II) was soon revoked, but it explains the initial assignments of black troops to the warmer Southwestern climate.

At least three derivations of the term "buffalo soldier" can be traced only through transfers from oral history into the literature of the West:

    1. Close-cropped, military haircuts emphasized the curly texture of the mens' hair; American Indians saw a similarity to the curly pelts of bison.

2. A black soldier, dressed in the dark blue, woolen uniform and sitting astride a dark, military-issue horse, if outlined on the horizon, looked much like a shaggy buffalo.

3. Although the standard winter military issue was dark blue, woolen overcoats, some black units were issued buffalo-hide coats.

Also, black troopers were often called "brunettes" or "nigger soldiers"[3]—the use of either term, particularly the latter, is not surprising given the times.

The terminology stuck, whatever the reasons, and the Ninth and Tenth U.S. Cavalries became the "buffalo soldiers" and proudly carried the name through the 1930s, when the last of the mounted troops were disbanded to become "armored" divisions. Later, the infantries would carry the designation.

It is not generally recognized by history that black troopers, fighting with whites, were the actual "heroes of San Juan Hill" under the leadership of Teddy Roosevelt. But, they were removed from the battle scene prior to the Rough Riders' famous charge, which was documented in paintings, movies, stories, and song. Similarly, many of the battles and skirmishes of the Indian wars were fought by "Negro" troops, encounters that resulted in an animosity between blacks and Indians.[4] That buffalo soldiers were often used to help capture and confine the Indians on reservations did nothing to ameliorate the situation.

Of interest is that many Indians called the soldiers "black white men" since they had never before seen people with skin as dark as that of these new captors and enemies. More warlike Indian groups—given the opportunity—either killed blacks or turned them into slaves. This ironic turn of events was omitted from most media accounts of the time, but it was noted with concern by African American soldiers and pilgrims who saw themselves as vulnerable.

3. From the Latin adjective "niger," meaning "black," the term has become the single most reviled racial epithet in modern use. Still, it was universally applied to black individuals in the American West and became a common term, often coupled with the person's proper name.

4. Black troopers and American Indians have a long history of animosity. One reason often cited by historians is that Chivington's massacre at Sand Creek—one of the most heinous in our history—was followed by black troopers from Fort Robinson, Nebraska, who were sent to clean up the battle site. Many Indians saw these troopers and equated them with the white cavalry who had actually carried out the mission. Magnified by the many fights between buffalo soldiers and Indians throughout the West, they were seldom allies in this period of western history.

Soldiers of the Ninth and Tenth Cavalries are shown working on a building in Fort Washakie, Wyoming, which was the central town on the Shoshone Indian reservation. Many of the buildings constructed by the soldiers still stand to this day. (Courtesy of the Wyoming State Museum and Archive, Cheyenne)

Military Experiments

In the late nineteenth and early twentieth centuries, the American Southwest was the scene of singular military experiments with firearms, clothing, transportation, and maneuvers. In Arizona, for instance, white cavalrymen were assigned to study the use of camels for desertlike warfare. An even more unique use was made of a nineteenth-century mechanical invention: the bicycle.

Units of the Tenth Cavalry from Fort Huachuca in Arizona and the Twenty-Fifth Infantry from Fort Missoula in Montana were assigned the task of testing bicycles as a means of military transportation. For a year,

(left and above) The James A. Moss group of the Twenty-Fifth Infantry Bicycle Corps from Fort Missoula, Montana, in Yellowstone National Park, October 1896. (Photographer: F. Jay Haynes; courtesy of the Haynes Foundation Collection, Montana Historical Society, Helena)

several groups started from the northern Rockies in Montana and toured southward, crossing Wyoming, Colorado, and New Mexico.

The experiment was, evidently, a failure, but it left some of the most intriguing photos of African American troopers of all time.

Negro-Seminole Scouts of the Twenty-Fourth Infantry

Runaway slaves often found their way west with the help of Florida Seminole Indians, who aided fugitive men and women in their flights. Many moved farther westward, avoiding major white settlements, some going as far as Nacimiento, Mexico.[5] In the 1870s, however, emancipation had

---

5. A series of legal pronouncements found in Mexican archives showed these runaways to be a constant source of irritation between proslavery forces in Texas and the Mexican government, which was reluctant to force their return. Only after emancipation did some begin to drift back north into Texas.

Original cabinet photograph (circa 1895) of Negro-Seminole Indian scouts, by J. M. Stotsenberg. (Courtesy of the Ben E. Pingenot Collection, Fort Clark, Brackettville, Texas.)

changed the racial atmosphere in the States, and these now racially mixed "black Indians" moved back across the border.

As a result of this migration into the Southwest, bands of Negro-Seminole Indians presented themselves to the U.S. military when it expanded its war against hostile Indians. They were astonished to find black Indians already there, trained and expert as frontier trackers and fighters who knew the territory. These men were inducted into the Twenty-Fourth Infantry at Fort Duncan, Texas.[6]

The unit, famed for the fierceness and loyalty of its members gained a

6. Often referred to in texts as "Negro-Seminole Indian scouts," these men, whose headquarters was located near Uvalde, Texas, prefer a designation which emphasizes their American Indian and military roots, freely acknowledging, however, that they are descendants of black soldiers who formed the first units.

Outfitted for the trail, this buffalo soldier, stationed on the Pine Ridge reservation in South Dakota, is wearing a working soldier's outfit of the times. (Courtesy of the Denver Public Library, Western History Collection, Colorado)

degree of fame by working as scouts for the (white) Fourth Cavalry as it chased bandits deep into Mexican territory. They led major assaults on hostile Indian groups across Texas, capturing some of the most warlike Kiowas and Comanches in the process.

In 1914, the assistant secretary of war requested that these scouts and their families be added to rosters of enrolled Seminoles and be subsequently granted deeded lands. The Interior Department denied the request, and these men ended their military careers largely unknown and unrecognized, disappearing into the shadows of western history.

COWHANDS
AND RANCH HANDS

No one knows when the first black man took up a lariat or applied for a piece of land to call his own under the open reaches of the sky west of the Mississippi River. One thing is certain, however, it was earlier than most think. Edmund Flagg, writing in 1838 of his earlier trip of two years to the the Far West, witnessed masters unloading barges of black slaves on the banks of the Missouri River in preparation for their journey to distant quarters of the Rocky Mountains and Plains territories.

Exact numbers are hard to derive, but it is safe to say that thousands of black men rode the trails of the American West from the mid-1800s through the early part of the twentieth century. If the thousands of military men, "exoduster" farmers, and other emigrants from the historic South are included in the count, there were, clearly, tens of thousands of African American men, women, and children in the West during the "cattle kingdom"

(left) "Spooked by Lightning," by Frederick Remington, displays the artist's continuing fascination with African Americans on the American frontier. As with his renderings of the military, Remington catches the danger and courage that pervaded cattle ranching in the nineteenth century. (Courtesy of the Gilcrease Museum, Tulsa, Oklahoma)

(top) Black jockeys racing horses in Cheyenne, Wyoming, near the turn of the century. Black cowboys were commonly employed as jockeys during this time. Like the Kentucky Derby, whose first decade was dominated by black jockeys, organized races in the West often hired black riders. (Courtesy of the Wyoming State Museum and Archive, Cheyenne)

(bottom) Tracy Thompson, bucking-horse champion, Idaho, circa 1900. (Courtesy of the Idaho State Historical Society, Boise)

(top and bottom right) African American cowhands at work in Wyoming and Colorado. (Courtesy of the American Heritage Center, LaFrantz Collection, University of Wyoming, Laramie)

years from 1860 to 1910—and this number does not take into consideration the people who moved northward into Canada.

Today, African Americans cowboys are portrayed in motion pictures, television programs, and magazine articles, but how the early historians could have missed the existence of this many people remains an intriguing mystery, as does the omission of black exploits in the stories and songs of the day.

Another misconception about African American cowhands is that they were all menial laborers. In fact, many were competent and skilled workers, certainly more experienced than the young men (usually teenagers) who worked under them. Coming, as many of these men did, from southern farms and plantations, they were especially skilled in training and vetting horses. When herding cattle, black cowhands often "rode point," which was a position of honor since the rider would be ahead of the dust clouds stirred up by the cattle.

Although often interpreted as a menial position, cooks were an important component of life on the range. They faced hungry and demanding cowboys daily. Cowboying was a tough and boring grind for the young men riding herd; and, with towns and settlements often tens of miles distant from the trail, they could become unruly and difficult to control. Consequently, cooks had to prepare a variety of appetizing meals as well as find ways of distracting youthful goings-on that could range from baking fresh fruit pies (a challenge since dry larders were the main source of "fresh" food) to making treats of candy and sweet drinks.

Cooks were employed for their combined skills in food storage and preparation, a knowledge of sources of comestibles on the trail, and a general

Black cooks were common on ranches in nearly every western state. (Courtesy of the Idaho State Historical Society, Boise)

This photograph of a man playing a guitar by some long-ago campsite captures the essence of a tradition with a long history. (From author's collection)

ability to control their rambunctious young comrades. Nearly every ranch of any size knows of multitalented black cooks who worked there—often for decades. Their contributions are a part of the historical record in virtually every place where cattle was king and the cowboy was knight-errant.

Another accomplishment of the African American cowboy was his musical talents. Cooks, especially, were often accomplished players of fiddles, harmonicas, and guitars. Most noteworthy cow-country musicians were black cowboys—contrary to the images of singing cowboys fostered in western films of the 1930s and 1940s. The popularized, legendary singing cowboy[1] was most likely a derivation of former slaves, now cowboys, who had brought with them the southern practice of using the musical sounds of a human voice to calm nervous cattle.

1. In motion pictures of the 1930s and 1940s, actor-singers Gene Autry and Roy Rogers were the most well known. Herb Jefferies, a black singer and producer of movies with black casts, preserved the historical origins of those men who sang to cattle to quiet them.

CHAPTER SIX

WOMEN OF THE WEST

I f the roles for black men were affected by the racism and prejudice of others, those for black women were even more affected. Given the societal restrictions placed upon women in general in the nineteenth century, it is truly surprising to find women who stood out in the crowd with their accomplishments. Although some chose a life-style that might be deemed less than salutary in nature—this was the West, after all—there were those who, through their success and determination, became the inspiration for other black women.

Some Positive Experiences

The number of documented ex-slave women who came west is small since most were the wives and daughters of men whose names—if recorded at

(*left*) Distorted stereotypes of African American women were perpetuated by images like this one in an 1800s stereograph. The figure is not a woman but a white man in blackface and wearing women's clothes to add to the "humor." A popular item of entertainment in the parlors of white Victorians was the stereoscope with which to view three-dimensional pictures. (From author's collection)

Accurate images of black women's appearance and roles were unknown to most whites of the times and apparently ignored when they were available. This attractive, well-dressed woman, who could afford to have her picture taken in a Los Angeles studio, circa 1890, is such an image. (From author's collection)

Teaching was one of the professions open to African American women, especially in remote parts of the West. Here, an unnamed woman stands on the Plains of northern Wyoming, circa 1890. (Courtesy of the J. Guthrie Nicholson, Jr., Collection, American Heritage Center, University of Wyoming, Laramie)

all—were forgotten over time. Mary Fields, however, was a noteworthy exception.

A native of Tennessee (born a slave circa 1832), Mary Fields moved to Montana in the company of Ursuline nuns after escaping slavery. Because she left the care of the nuns when she was a teenager, her life in not recorded in great detail. What is known, however, ranks her among the most interesting, individualistic, and determined women of the era.

Six feet tall and weighing two hundred pounds, with a girth to match, she brooked little challenge in her various jobs. Barkeeper, mail carrier,[1] brawler, whorehouse owner, and a cigar-smoking, Wells Fargo shotgun rider in Montana and northern Wyoming (maybe even swinging north

1. One of the more common occupations of early black settlers in the West was that of postmaster. Apparently, this was not a job coveted by resident whites, probably due to its long hours and low pay. Many areas of the West, however, could boast of the black men and women who opened post offices in far-flung settlements.

Mary Fields, bar owner, postmistress, shotgun rider for Wells Fargo Express, on the streets of Miles City, Montana, circa 1895. Of the five known images of Fields, only this photo shows her with a shotgun. (Courtesy of the Ursuline Centre, Great Falls, Montana)

into Canada on occasion), she was a composite of personality traits necessary for survival in those days and places. Her high spirits and tough lifestyle cast her as a truly unforgettable character of the American West.

If one state has remained in people's imagination as symbolic of the Rocky Mountain West, it is surely Colorado. Prospering and growing with the gold and silver booms of the mid-nineteenth century, Colorado saw a wild mélange of railroaders, mountain men, cowboys, whores, ranchers,

Mary Fields became a successful businesswoman in times when both gender and color limited opportunities. The photo shows Fields in one of her characteristic hats, behind her favorite horse, circa 1895, probably in Miles City, Montana. (Courtesy of the Ursuline Centre, Great Falls, Montana)

miners, hoteliers, lawmakers, soldiers, guides, hunters, entrepreneurs, philanthropists, teachers, newspaper editors, ministers, and more. And all these were black.

Among those who dedicated their lives to the betterment of others, in ways most people would find difficult to emulate, was "Aunt" Clara Brown.

Born a slave in Spotsylvania County, Virginia, in 1806, she was sold as a three-year-old to a Mr. Brown from Logan, Kentucky. Although the history is cloudy, she found her way to Kansas Territory as an "exoduster" in the great out-migration of black southerners during the late 1850s, apparently heading west with those caught up in the Rocky Mountain gold rush. Noted for her kindness and gentle nature, she was often referred to as "the angel of the Rockies" during her travel toward what is now Colorado.

Central City, the destination of her wagon train, was a rough-and-tumble boomtown in the Rockies. As a town it was a more suitable place for rugged miners and their ways of life than for a fortyish black woman who wanted to found an African Methodist Episcopal church, be active in Sunday school programs, and acquire property.

(left) "Aunt" Clara Brown. Colorado pioneer in the gold-mining towns of the Rockies. (Courtesy of the Colorado State Historical Society, Denver)

(right) Mary Ellen Pleasant. (Courtesy of the San Francisco Public Library, San Francisco, California)

A frugal woman who kept her own counsel, she began to acquire inexpensive land around Central City as well as around the cattle and Indian town of Denver, consisting at the time of little more than canvas-covered buildings and tepees around Cherry Creek.

She frequently grubstaked miners who had no other means of support while they looked for gold in the mountains west of Denver, and was repaid handsomely for her kindness and generosity by those who struck pay dirt. She used any profits to continue her philanthropy among the needy and to increase her landholdings.

Nature and Lady Luck were not kind to Clara Brown. In one of the periodic great floods that sweep down out of the foothills west of Denver,

A typical occupation for an African American woman in the West was that of midwife. Sybil Harber achieved prominence for her skill as a midwife in her hometown of Lakeview, Oregon, in the late 1800s. (Courtesy of the Oregon Historical Society, Portland)

the records of her landholdings were washed away. She could not prove ownership and subsequently lost title to much of her property. In addition, there were dishonest business rivals who found her vulnerable to their unscrupulous deals, especially when her property records were lost. Eventually, she had nothing left but her kind and charitable ways, but no one whom she had helped at one time or another let her suffer the privations of hunger or lack of love.

Whether rich or poor, landholder or not, "Aunt" Clara Brown became one of the true legends of the Rocky Mountains in the past century.

Mary Ellen Pleasant, an early pioneering woman, was better known as "Mammy Pleas." She resented the appellation, considering it an overly familiar form of address. Called an "angel of the West" by many for her work with troubled and abused women, men, and children, she was a mercurial businesswomen known far more widely than in her home base of San Francisco in the late 1800s.

A self-proclaimed capitalist, she was partners with Thomas Bell, cofounder of the first Bank of California. As a businesswoman, Mary Ellen was most likely cunning, cynical, and calculating, but she was also soft-hearted by nature in helping many individuals in need of financial or personal support. An intriguing rumor: she may have murdered Thomas Bell and plotted to kill his foster son.

Her statement, "I am a theater in myself," was a self-admission of having a complex character. She used large sums of money (how and where obtained is uncertain) to aid fugitive slaves and freedmen. She fed them, found occupations for them, and financially backed them in numerous small businesses. She was also a leader in the protection of abused women, building and supporting safe havens for them in California.

Whatever her true motivations, Mary Ellen Pleasant carved herself an indelible niche in western American history.

Some Adverse Experiences

Traditionally, the criminal stereotype is a male. Throughout history, the majority of incarcerated individuals in North America—and the world in all probability—have been men. However, there have been black women who were apprehended and sentenced to prison.

Eliza Stewart was sentenced in 1899 to the territorial prison at Laramie, Wyoming, for shooting at her paramour—and missing. A large woman, recorded in prison documents as "weighing over 200 pounds," Eliza served time in the equivalent of a federal penitentiary for an assault for which few, if any, white women were ever charged. She served one year, nine months, and was released.

Caroline Hayes was sentenced a second time to the penitentiary for one year, nine months for an unspecified crime. Oddly, a mere two weeks after her release, she was again arrested for stealing two fifty-cent blankets from a local store. This time she was incarcerated in the local jail and then sent home to Cheyenne, Wyoming.

The issue, of course, was not that these crimes were particularly heinous or a major threat to public safety. Some women were put in jail for stealing

left) Eliza Stewart was known as "Big Jack" to her friends and comrades. (Courtesy of the Wyoming State Museum and Archive, Cheyenne)

(right) Caroline Hayes (also Winfield), a native of Ohio, served time in the Wyoming territorial prison in Laramie. (Courtesy of the Wyoming State Museum and Archive, Cheyenne)

bread or small articles of clothing. Clearly, their crime was that of "stepping out of bounds," by not heeding social expectations of standards of behavior set by the white majority for both black men and women.

Few women—regardless of skin color—served full terms in these prisons. Most were released after a few months because of ill health, for good behavior, or for being pregnant.[2]

2. How a woman could become pregnant while in a territorial prison, completely isolated from wardens, guards, and other prisoners is a reasonable question. Unless they were pregnant prior to being imprisoned, the answer is obvious: they weren't that isolated. Whatever the stated reasons may have been, officials were apparently eager to release their female charges as soon as possible.

Fashionably dressed, this woman posed for the camera lens of O. E. Aultman in Trinidad, Colorado, in the late 1800s. (Courtesy of the Colorado State Historical Society, Denver)

The Aultman Photographs

One of the longest lasting photographic studios in the American West is that of O. E. Aultman, in Trinidad, Colorado.[3] Both O. E. and Trinidad are worthy subjects for discussion.

The town, cosied up near the foot of Raton Pass, nudges the New Mexico/Colorado border. The pass, well known to the Indians, marks a geological cleft in the southern Rocky Mountains, an otherwise solid bar-

3. The O. E. Aultman collection is housed in the Colorado State Historical Society in Denver. It contains about five thousand images—mostly glass plate negatives—ranging over a period of nearly one hundred years and is a priceless document of the West.

This woman, dressed in typical nurses' uniform at the turn of the century, apparently worked in the Trinidad, Colorado, area. (From author's collection)

rier to passage between the two states. Apparently, the Don Juan Oñate expedition of 1598 followed the pass through the mountains some twenty-two years before the Pilgrims landed at Plymouth Rock. Later, the area became a safe haven for every badman in the West and home to miners from Greece and England. Each in their time, railroads, stagecoach service, men with their oxteams and wagons, cowboys and their herds, and highways, old and new, have passed through this funnel-shaped area heading north toward more populated territory. Trinidad became a natural gathering site that brought together laborers and pioneers of various beliefs and racial backgrounds a hundred years ago. Many travelers lingered momentarily, but most moved on; only a few descendants of those who did stay have persevered until modern times.

O. E. Aultman opened his photographic studio in 1889 and began one of the most remarkable collections of what we today call an "ethnographic record" in the country. These photos preserve, for all time, images of the people who lived in this small, ethnically rich town in a hollow of the Rockies.

Photographs in this collection record the varied occupations of African Americans, Japanese, Mexicans, American Indians, and more. These images are carefully posed studio photographs, in contrast to the inexpensive, casual snapshots associated with itinerant photographers passing the time between more lucrative assignments. Aultman became known for his willingness to accept a subsidy for his work. In this instance, his fee for a photo session would be paid by someone who wished to subsidize the project. His photographs are therefore not ordinarily identified by the names of his subjects, but rather by the names of the individuals who paid him for his work.

The nineteenth-century African American women captured on film by O. E. Aultman and reproduced here are unknown and unnamed, but they represent a selected gallery of the varied roles played by black women in the early days of the West. (All Aultman photographs shown are courtesy of the Colorado State Historical Society, Denver.)

THE ADVENTURERS

I t all began with York:[1]

. . . and one of the men had spread the report of our having with us a man perfectly black, whose hair was short and curled . . .

We assured him it was true, and sent for York. Le Borgne was very much surprised at his appearance, examined him closely, and spit on his finger and rubbed the skin in order to wash off the paint; nor was it

1. More accurately, it began with the Moor, "Little Steven" (Estevan), who was most likely the first black man seen by Indians in what became the American Southwest. Often referred to as "the discoverer of Texas," he was probably a runaway from a wrecked slave ship off the coast of Florida in the 1520s. As with many after him, he was aided in his escape by Seminole Indians who helped him find his way west, ending in Mexico. From there, he joined Spanish expeditions into Indian lands, searching for the legendary Seven Cities of Cíbola, the cities of gold, and may have been with Pánfilo de Narváez's search through Florida in 1528. Crossing what is now part of Arizona, Texas, and New Mexico, he was a member of several expeditions and was certainly an item of wonder—akin to York's reception—when he appeared on Indian horizons.

(left) A Currier and Ives print showing York, a slave of William Clark, unloading boats on the Platte River, circa 1885. (From author's collection)

until the negro uncovered his head and showed his short hair, that Le Borgne could be persuaded that he was not a painted white man . . .

The object which appeared to astonish the Indians most was Captain Clark's servant York, a remarkably stout, strong negro. They had never seen a being of that color, and therefore flocked round him to examine the extraordinary monster. By way of amusement, he told them that he had once been a wild animal, and caught and tamed by his master; and to convince them showed them feats of strength which, added to his looks, made him more terrible than we wished him to be.

(Lewis 1904, vol. 1, pt. 2, 185)

Little more than what is noted above is written about York from first-hand experience. York was a slave of William Clark,[2] and accompanied his master and Meriweather Lewis throughout their mapping and explorations in 1804–6 of the Northwest Territory, what is now the Dakotas, Montana, Idaho, and Washington. He was clearly an important member of the first major survey party of the American West.

Records indicate that he was especially skilled with horses; and, although not a translator for the expedition, it seems that he had an "ear" for American Indian languages. York had very dark skin ("black as a bear," wrote Pierre Antoine Tabeau, trader with the Arikaras) and was personable and an attractive curiosity to the Indians with whom Lewis and Clark had to deal.

Apocrypha abound concerning this man. For example, he was a juggler and gymnast (probably true), a master of several Indian tongues (maybe true, but unlikely), larger than normal in size for his time (probably true), handsome beyond all belief (no one knows), and popular with Indian women—to the point of leaving several offspring in his wake (anyone's guess).

Clearly, York left an indelible mark on the memories of those who knew him, as is evident in popular histories of the Lewis and Clark expedition.

Many shadowy figures passed through history unknown and their ex-

2. York was the "body servant" of Clark, a term that signified the assignment of a young slave to his equally young master for companionship. Family records indicate that York, the son of slaves, Rose and Old York, was given to Clark by his father in 1799. The association lasted until Clark hired him out to another slaveholder, apparently because the friendship had ended. York was freed sometime after 1811 and, according to varying stories, either died in the South or—a more traditional western version—returned to the West, joined the Crow Indians and died in honor sometime between 1815 and 1819 as one of them.

Unknown mountain man photographed probably in northern California in the 1880s. (Courtesy of the California State Library, Sacramento)

ploits unrecorded. Others merely slipped into a temporary silence only to be resurrected by historians.

Isaiah Dorman: Guide, Translator, Hero

Ever since the advent of motion pictures, the movie western has been part of America's mass culture. Some western motifs have received more attention than others. As an example: nearly thirty films about Gen. George Armstrong Custer's "last stand" at the battle on the Little Bighorn River in Montana have depicted this monumental defeat at the hands of superior Indian forces. In none of these movies is there the slightest suggestion that a black man was there. The fact of the matter is that one was there: Isaiah Dorman, who perished in the battle. He was with Maj. Marcus A. Reno's contingent of troopers, engaged in a defensive fight with the Indians some three miles south of where the main battle occurred.

Serving as guides from the earliest days of discovery explorations and western travel, black men accompanied U.S. geological mapping surveys, expeditions to Yellowstone country, and others such as the Lewis and Clark expedition; they were a part of U.S. military maneuvers throughout the West. Nearly as common as black cowboys, these guides, outfitters, hunt-

(left) Isaiah Dorman's gravestone marks the site of his death at the battle of the Little Big Horn. Although virtually all other death sites at the national monument were given markers prior to the 1940s, Dorman's was put in place in the 1950s. His was the last stone to be erected. (Photo by J. W. Ravage)

(right) Throughout the era of western exploration, Black men—such as this one—were commonly used as laborers, guides, and porters. This photograph was taken in Montana Territory, circa 1880. (Courtesy of the United States Geological Survey Photographic Archives, Denver, Colorado)

ers, provisioners, cooks, and foremen are noted in accounts of the time. And many were photographed.

In Isaiah Dorman's case, however, there are no authenticated photographs of him, which is surprising since he served with General Custer and was part of various private and military expeditions for a number of years. And Custer was photographed with hundreds of his friends and acquaintances over most of his military life. The general was an obvious "media personality," and appears to have relished his appearance in photographs.

What little is known about Dorman derives from a few short texts about Custer's "Black White Man" who accompanied him on several military and personal forays. The texts refer to Dorman's skill with Plains Indian languages and his repeated hiring by the government to lead expeditions as a translator and guide. A significant detail: his pay scale exceeded that of the troopers by a factor of three (Carroll 1971:360). He must have possessed extraordinary skills for a man of his times.

Unidentified black guide and Indians, circa 1873, in the Yellowstone area, photographed by Thomas O'Sullivan. (Courtesy of the United States Geological Survey Photographic Archives, Denver, Colorado)

Thomas O'Sullivan, a contract photographer for the U.S. government, documented several mapping and military expeditions in the 1870s throughout the Southwest, Montana Territory, and the Yellowstone area prior to its being set aside as a national park. One of his photographs is of a young black man and what may be Apache guides. Could the man be Dorman? No one knows for sure.

The man wears the traditional garb of guides of the time, and has two of Dorman's three known physical attributes: a very wide nose and a large

(above) Members of Custer's Yellowstone expedition. Note the man standing behind the group by a tent who could be Isaiah Dorman. (Courtesy of the South Dakota State Historical Society, Pierre)

(top right) Digitally enhanced close-up of the figure by a tent in the photograph of Custer's Yellowstone expedition members.

(bottom right) If an image of Isaiah Dorman is to be found anywhere it is probably in this photograph of Custer's Seventh Cavalry taken within a year of the battle at the Little Big Horn. Dorman may well be one of the men on white horses. (Courtesy of the National Archives, Washington, D.C.)

chest. Dorman also had an enlarged thumb on his left hand, which may or may not show in the photograph. This detail is not clear; the man might have moved his thumb as the shutter snapped. Sitting behind this man is yet another individual who might be Dorman.

Another photograph that may include the elusive Dorman was taken on the Custer Yellowstone expedition of 1874. The figure in the background may be Dorman. A documented photograph of Dorman may never be found, but the tantalizing possibility—albeit remote—is worth the search.

Throughout his career George Armstrong Custer had numerous relationships with African Americans as military aides and civilian camp employees.

(above) Members of the Clarence King survey party, mapping the fortieth parallel, circa 1868–70. (Courtesy of the United States Geological Survey Photographic Archives, Denver, Colorado)

(top left) Custer was taken prisoner in the Civil War and incarcerated in the South. This Matthew Brady photograph shows him and Lieutenant Washington, a confederate, alongside an unidentified black child. (Courtesy of the Library of Congress, Washington, D.C.)

(bottom left) The Custers and Lucy (last name unrecorded), their cook. The photograph was taken at Fort Lincoln, Montana Territory. (Courtesy of the North Dakota State Historical Society, Bismarck)

The Custers nearly always employed black cooks and handymen. Effie Custer described Lucy in her diaries. Another black cook, Mary Kercherval (see next chapter), was in their employ at the time of the famous battle; she and Effie stayed behind at Fort Lincoln.

Guides and Hunters

In the late 1800s, the U.S. Congress subsidized several expeditions of discovery in the West. They were to focus mainly on geologic formations,

Members of Ferdinand Hayden's expedition of 1869–70, probably in southern Wyoming Territory or northern Colorado. (Courtesy of the American Heritage Center, University of Wyoming, Laramie)

with a strong emphasis on an area's economic potential. Lewis and Clark's expedition was merely the most famous of these journeys. Others, particularly those led by Dr. Ferdinand Hayden and John Wesley Powell, were equally important as scientific ventures.

In the 1870s Ferdinand Hayden led several mapping expeditions of

On Hayden's expedition of 1871, Joe Clark, seen in this close-up, was a hunter assigned to the crew. He is mentioned several times in the logbooks of the expedition kept by its surgeon, Dr. A. C. Peale. (Photo by W. H. Jackson; courtesy of the U.S. Geological Survey Photographic Archives, Denver, Colorado)

Yellowstone and the Gallatin Forest in what is now southern Montana. The main job of the expedition, composed of nearly fifty men, was to record the geology, flora, and fauna of an area that would later become Montana, Wyoming, Idaho, and parts of Colorado. In the Hayden expedition photograph are a General Cook (in the robe), Thomas Moran (seated near the tent), and the provisioner of the group: the black man whose name is not recorded. His job was to supply and maintain tents and firearms, tend to horses and livestock, and provide fresh meat. Moran would find a scenic view that he would recreate as one of his most famous paintings, *Mount of the Holy Cross*.

Members of the Tenth Cavalry from Ft. Huachuca are even less well known than some of the individuals mentioned in this chapter. These men

were part of a contingent assigned to map, for the first time, an area that would later become Yellowstone National Park. Congress knew that this assignment would be dangerous: angry Indians did not want what they interpreted as an incursion into their homelands. There were no national park rangers, obviously, so the men were specifically commissioned to safe-guard the surveyors' and scientists' lives. (Nearly a decade later, Harry Yount would become the first official park ranger.) Of note: these photographs of the guardian "rangers" have never before been printed.

(top left) The Tenth Cavalry from Fort Huachuca in Arizona was assigned to protect the first mapping expeditions of the Yellowstone area, circa 1880. (Courtesy of the Teton County Historical Society, Jackson, Wyoming)

(bottom left) Black "rangers" from Fort Huachuca, Arizona, assigned to the Yellowstone area, circa 1880. Note the marshalls' badges and the woman. (Courtesy of the Teton County Historical Society, Jackson, Wyoming)

TO THE COAST

California

California has a long and varied history that incorporates the experiences of African Americans who ventured into what would be later called "the Golden State" from its days as part of the Spanish domain to its rowdy gold-rush era and then through the "cowboy kingdom" years of the early twentieth century. Black citizens were active participants in Spanish territorial life; many were descendants of Moors, a vigorous North African people who conquered Spain in the eighth century and ruled there for five hundred years.

The "California or Bust (by Gum)" fever carried across racial and economic lines. By 1850 black men, women, and children numbered about 1,000 out of a population of 93,000, with another 1,000 or so individuals of mixed ancestry (referred to as "mulattos" in some records). As previously mentioned, this 1 to 3 percent figure is relatively constant in records that exist from many western territories and states. By 1900 or so, about 1,500 farms were owned by "colored settlers" throughout California.

(left) Unidentified travelers whose slogan was "California by Gum," circa 1890–1892, in Weaverville, California. Note the weapons worn and carried by the driver, an indication of uneasy times. (Photograph by William Wax; courtesy of Peter Palmquist, Arvata, California.)

Nevada City, California, in 1852. Northwest of Sacramento lay some of the richest gold-bearing soils in North America. California's forty-niners were of every possible physical description and age. These people are at work in a forested area. (Courtesy of the California State Library, Sacramento, California)

The Gold Rush and Slavery

By the early 1850s about 1,000 slaves lived in California (Lapp 1977:3). Nearly all were indentured to their masters, who had brought them west. Many were promised, or harbored the expectation, that they might earn their freedom after a period of time.

By the 1860s, some were working on steamers or herding cattle for livestock owners. There were undoubtedly some who had fled to areas along the coast. The California legal system was inconsistent when it came to either enforcing the southern laws of slavery or allowing African Americans to function as nominally free men. Judges in their ruling on the status of individuals declaring themselves free without the benefit of legal southern documentation were erratic in enforcing the out-of-state regulations. Some people were granted freedom; others were not.

Eventually, California passed its own fugitive slave law, which stated that anyone who entered the state either as a runaway or with his or her master prior to the state's joining the Union in 1852 was, indeed, mere property and could be jailed, fined, or, if a runaway, returned to the owner. Anyone arriving after the statehood date was free.

Given the varied interpretations of the law by the courts, *de-facto* slavery was a part of California's history for many years after the law was passed.

One of the unwritten laws upheld by gold miners was that if a person discovered gold it was that person's property. A problem arose when certain work arrangements seemed to circumvent this law. If a slave discovered gold while prospecting for his master, it was the master who claimed ownership. Some of the prospectors—those without "helpers" who considered this violation of the "law" unfair—joined forces and made slave owners move out of the area or discontinue the practice entirely. Simultaneously, and inconsistently, they declared any claims filed by African Americans invalid.

Many of the men who became independent chose to stay and send money back home to buy out the indentures of family members and friends. California was admitted to the Union as a free state, creating legal problems for those who had retained their status as slaves because they had entered the state prior to its achieving statehood. The new state constitution did not address the issue, although early legislation discriminated severely and specifically against Mexicans, Asians, and African Americans.

Some slave owners simply put their property up for sale, hoping that buyers could be found. Some left for remote areas in Oregon and Canada. Others took what money they could from their slaves and released them.

Runaways and the newly freed also left the state because of widespread discrimination. Many moved north to British Columbia and areas around Vancouver Island. So many left that San Francisco newspapers ran editorials that criticized punitive legislation and encouraged them to reconsider and return to the state (Lapp 1977:13). Most did not.

Eventually, however, slavery issues and the fugitive slave law became irrelevant when no more slave holders entered the state.

The contagion of gold fever spread rapidly; infected individuals reacted with an intensity seldom seen except on Wall Street. Farmers, lawyers, doctors, dentists, and "loose women," to name only a few, caught the disease and left for the California goldfields with fevered visions of finding and working a mother lode.

Alvin Coffey, born a slave, was one of several who accompanied their masters to the goldfields of northern California to help with mining operations. As with many other men in the goldfields, Coffey stayed with his master even though California was "free" territory. Although no one knows for certain what motivated these men to stay in such a punishing system, the arroyos of the Golden State may have been too seductive an attraction. For whatever reason, Coffey (who came to the region in 1849) and others

(top) Alvin Coffey, California pioneer. (Courtesy of the Northern California Center for Afro American History Museum, Oakland)

Photograph of a prospector working in the California goldfields, taken circa 1855. (Courtesy of the California State Library, Sacramento)

(top) In all probability, a white master with his slaves (note man and woman in background), circa 1850, in northern California. (Courtesy of the California State Library, Sacramento)

Mining in northern California, mid-1850s. Asians, as well as African Americans, were common laborers in the goldfields. (Courtesy of the California State Library, Sacramento)

B 2005 Lucky Baldwin's Thoroughbreds San Gabriel, Cal., imported from the South in 1886.

The caption to this photograph reads, "Lucky Baldwin's Thoroughbreds . . . imported from the South in 1886." These people were workers for the new agricultural industry in northern California. (Courtesy of the California State Library, Sacramento)

worked their way to freedom, buying out their indentures with the yellow grains they sluiced from the streams and hills. After purchasing his freedom, Coffey settled in the Red Bluffs area of the state.

The California gold rush was a precursor of other such responses to finding the yellow metal in British Columbia, the Yukon, and Alaska. African Americans were among the many who joined in the pursuit of fame and fortune in the north.

Beyond the Goldfields

The needs of the manual labor market in California attracted a wide assortment of workers. Men, women, and children arrived to meet those needs, as represented by "Lucky Baldwin's Thoroughbreds," who were brought in from southern states in 1886 to work as domestics and field hands on farms near Sacramento and in central California.

Others came to work as cowhands. Rolf Logan is a good example of a

(top) Rolf Logan on his horse, Roundup, circa 1890. Well known throughout northern and central California, Logan was a pioneering cowboy and homesteader. (Courtesy of the California State Library, Sacramento)

Rolf Logan branding cattle. (Courtesy of the California State Library, Sacramento)

(top left) Railroad workers, circa 1890. Men were needed as gandy dancers to construct railbeds, set the wooden ties, and lay the rails. This need was a common source of employment. (Courtesy of the City of Oakland, California)

(bottom left) William Shorrey, sailor, businessman, owner of a fleet of ships that serviced the west coast of the United States as far north as Alaska. (Courtesy of the Northern California Center for Afro American History Museum, Oakland)

(above) Employees of the Palace Hotel, San Francisco, circa 1890. (Courtesy of the California State Library, Sacramento)

northern California cowboy of the 1800s. He rode the range on his trusty steed Roundup and performed the same duties expected of every other ranch hand in the West.

There was work on the railroads to meet a variety of needs. Some men became shipowners. Both men and women found work in hotels.

Then there were the bandits and badmen.

(above) Charlie Rodriguez, "bandit," was born in Jamaica. He concentrated his activities in the Santa Cruz area in the mid- 1800s, ultimately serving three terms in San Quentin State Prison. (Courtesy of the Miriam Matthews Collection, California African-American Museum, Los Angeles)

(top and bottom right) Unidentified early residents of California. It is apparent from their clothes and other details that these families are members of the middle class. (From author's collection)

But, people raised families and prospered.

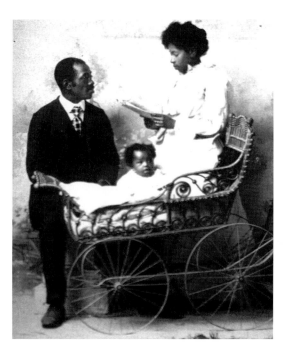

Dr. and Mrs. Monroe. He was a physician in Los Angeles, circa 1900. By the late 1800s, occupations that had been denied most African Americans became more accessible, as did the social positions that came with them. (Courtesy of the Miriam Matthews Collection, California African-American Museum, Los Angeles)

Although it is generally held that Thomas Bradley, elected in the 1980s, was the first African American mayor of the largest city west of New York City, Fernando Reyes actually holds that distinction. Reyes's family continued to own property in southern California until the mid-twentieth century.

Fernando Reyes, circa 1880, the first black mayor of Los Angeles. His racial heritage was Mexican/African American. He ruled the burgeoning pueblo in the late part of that century. (Courtesy of the Miriam Matthews Collection, California African-American Museum, Los Angeles)

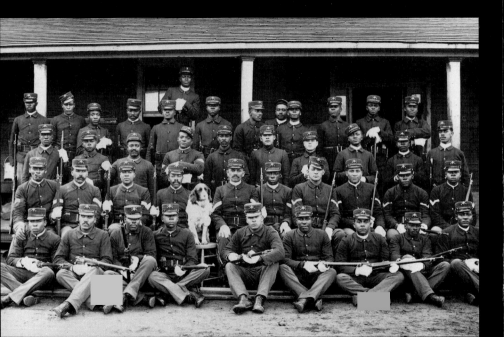

PLAINS STATES
Oklahoma, Kansas, South Dakota, Nebraska

Oklahoma

Individuals of African descent entered the region that is now Oklahoma with the first Spanish explorers of the continent. When Coronado
and his men crossed Texas in 1541, they also journeyed into the lands
immediately to the east. As historians have noted, "blackamoors" and "Ibe-
rians" were with exploratory expeditions to the Americas, including
Columbus's first voyages.[1] They were also with Juan de Oñate in his 1601
campaign. Historian Arthur Tolson (1974:8) notes that there were approximately two hundred Spanish towns in America, with a total population that included about forty thousand blacks and uncounted numbers of

1. From Columbus's crew to the men with Ponce de Leon and the Spanish expeditions of
the sixteenth century to the followers of Simon Bolivar, a creole who liberated northern
South America from Spanish rule, black individuals were among those who were making
history.

(left) The Twenty-Fourth Infantry at Fort Reno, Oklahoma Territory, circa
1890. There are even fewer known photographs of the two "Negro infantries,"
the Twenty-Fourth and Twenty-Fifth than there are of black cavalry units. Both
infantries were formed after the Civil War. (Courtesy of Fort Sill Museum,
Oklahoma)

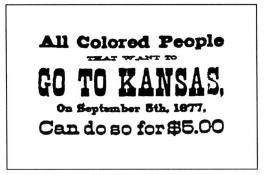

"mestizos" and "mulattos." Later, the French would also be in the area, bringing with them their domestic servants from Jamaica, Haiti, and the West Indies.

Legal possession of this area occurred in 1803 when Congress acquired it as part of the Louisiana Purchase. In 1817, the federal government began a removal of the Five Civilized Tribes from the area. This purge lasted for twenty-five years, resulting in a dramatic out-migration to Indian Territory of Cherokee, Chickasaw, Choctaw, Creek, and Seminole Indians. Southern Indian groups, many of whom brought their black slaves with them, moved into the eastern part of the territory; and after the Civil War, freed slaves began to arrive.

Kansas

The result of all this activity was that by the mid-1800s both Oklahoma and Kansas were homeland to a high percentage of African Americans in their population bases. Worldwide attention was drawn to the "exodusters" who, for a decade, flowed into the territory in large numbers. Over 15,000 African Americans, for example, settled in Kansas in one year, 1880 (Everitt 1937:197).

Promoters traveled to southern states to encourage former slaves to move to this new land of opportunity. The objective of the campaign was to benefit both African Americans and the white entrepreneurs who were selling land, needed a labor force, and saw the political power that could arise out of population growth and eventual statehood. Breaking one stereotype of the times, local white landowners generally accepted—even welcomed— these new emigrants to a place that needed people. Most of these new citizens became tillers of the soil; others became cowboys and ranch hands.

Black cowboys in California *(top)* and Kansas *(bottom)*. These cabinet cards, a popular photographic format in the nineteenth-century, illustrate the contributions of African Americans to an expanding America. (Top: from author's collection; bottom: courtesy of the California State Library, Sacramento)

Of more recent historical note: one Kansas town, Nicodemus[2], in Graham County, grew, nearly died, and was reborn in the 1980s as a retirement home for black families from the East Coast. Others, like Kansas City, Topeka, and Atchison, for example, began as black settlements and have prospered to this day.

Farmers in the South were concerned about the diminishing labor supply associated with this exodus to the flat farmlands of the Plains. This concern coupled with the incendiary issue in the U.S. Congress over whether to admit Kansas to the Union as a slave state created an environment that led to passage of the Homestead Act of 1862 and the subsequent race by hundreds of people for free land on which to settle. The records and photographs of that historical event reveal that there were virtually no African Americans—or American Indians—among the participants.[3]

South Dakota

Not all black pioneers in the West worked with cattle or on the railroads. In Hot Springs, South Dakota, for example, African Americans were brought in from Chicago to staff hotels. Others were looking for a place where they could continue the agrarian way of life they had left back in the East or the South. Although Rocky Mountain homesteads were not suited to plowing and planting, large tracts of what are now the Dakotas, Nebraska, and Kansas were excellent prospects for farming.

THE BLAKEY SAGA

In 1843, a woman, three sons (Isaac, Spencer, and John) and one daughter arrived on the slave docks of New Orleans. The members of this family were probably captured Bantus.

The family was immediately broken up; Isaac (age 12) and John (age 10) were sold to a man named Blakey of Forest Green, Missouri.

The rest of the family were sold to "Master White" of Natchez, Mississippi.

---

2. Nicodemus was named after a Biblical king and also a slave who had bought his freedom and become a respected social and political leader of the mid-1800s.

3. As in the Oklahoma land rush, the Tenth Cavalry was assigned to stop "sooners" (those who tried to get to the free lands ahead of—hence, sooner than—others) from being successful in Riverton, Wyoming, when Chief Washakie was persuaded by the federal government to let non-Indian homesteaders claim lands.

The two brothers had worked approximately four years on the Blakey plantation when Isaac escaped to the North, where he joined the Union forces. Too young to flee or fight, John was left behind. Isaac served three years, nine months in the army.

Isaac married Rachel LeFebure in Natchez, Mississippi in the late 1800s on his return from fighting in the Civil War. The couple moved to Missouri, produced eighteen children, eleven boys and seven girls. (Later, in 1905, Rachel would move to Yankton, South Dakota. Grandsons Ted, Nate, and Spencer Blakey were the nucleus of a black population in Yankton that lasts to this day.)

After the war, Isaac had returned to New Orleans to search for the remainder of the family—which had taken the name White—and finally tracked them down in Natchez. Shortly thereafter, he moved the regenerated family—now, the Blakey-White families—to Forest Green, where John had remained.

Around 1900, Isaac and his son Henry from a second marriage, hearing of the "promised land" of the Dakotas, moved to what is now South Dakota, near Yankton. It was an unsettled time, in many respects, since the area had undergone a series of racially inspired uprisings against the Twenty-Fifth Infantry, stationed at Fort Randall, near Yankton.[4] Consequently, most black emigrants settled on farms, isolated from the predominantly white communities.

Yankton seems to have had a somewhat easier environment in which these men and women could live without arousing racial anxieties. The Blakey branch of the Blakey-White family chose this part of South Dakota as their home ground.

Robert Bailey

On the far western edge of South Dakota, near Edgemont, there gathered yet another pioneering family, the Baileys. Robert Bailey served with the Tenth Cavalry in Wyoming and Nebraska as well as in the Spanish-American War. After returning from the Philippines, he served out the remainder of his enlistment with other black troops at Fort D. A. Russell in Chey-

---

4. The black infantry was posted near the Yankton Indian reservation to carry out a typical assignment: guard Indians on the reserve and keep white settlers from causing problems. Some infantrymen were assigned to guard Sitting Bull and the 160 Hunkpapas who came back from Saskatchewan in 1881 to be imprisoned for two years.

(top) In 1905, Mary Fristo Blakey eloped with Henry Blakey, leaving Salisbury, Missouri, and moving to Yankton, South Dakota. She is shown here with her son, Arthur Raymond. (Courtesy Ted Blakey, Yankton, South Dakota)

Brothers James and Zacharias (Bud) Blakey selling vegetables in Yankton near the turn of the century. (Courtesy of Ted Blakey, Yankton, South Dakota)

Robert Bailey, circa 1890, in his Sunday best, shortly after he had homesteaded in western Nebraska. (Courtesy of William Bailey III, Edgemont, South Dakota)

enne, Wyoming. When he mustered out, Robert decided to stay in the country he had learned to love.

Robert and his wife, Ella Mae, moved from Georgia to South Dakota in 1909, a time when the African American exodus to the Great Plains was at its highest peak. In order to amass more acreage, both of them homesteaded separate, but adjoining, claims and began to "prove up on them," in compliance with the law.

Later, Robert went back to Georgia where the couple had left their children while they built a house and established themselves. They raised seven children, all of then in the Edgemont area.

Bill Bailey[5] (William B. Bailey III) was one of Robert and Ella Mae's

5. Robert Bailey was one of three brothers who served in various divisions of the buffalo soldiers around the turn of the century. The family tells of a wandering nephew, young Bill, who was always a concern to his father. It was reported that Robert was always searching for his son, a young man not prone to keep regular hours. The lament was so well known to the family that Bill's niece, Pearl Bailey, based one of her most famous songs on the theme: "Won't You Come Home, Bill Bailey?"

children. Born around 1903, his life was colorful and varied. Among his exploits: a buffalo soldier stationed at Fort Robinson, Nebraska, in the last years of the calvary and the formation of what is today called "armored" divisions (tanks and motorized troops); the noted wanderer; and the first African American to own a casino in Reno, Nevada.

Standing six and one-half feet tall and nearing 100 years in age, Bill Bailey is still an imposing figure.

THE KERCHERVAL FAMILY

In 1873, young Mary Kercherval and her son Charles traveled to the Dakotas with the Seventh Cavalry. Mary was George Armstrong Custer's personal cook,[6] who began working for the Custers at Fort Dodge, Kansas. Later, the two would accompany the Seventh to Fort Rice, Dakota Territory, where Custer's forces protected engineers of the Northern Pacific Railroad as they platted a new railbed from Bismarck to the Yellowstone area.

Charles was assigned the duties of caring for Custer's horses and dogs; the general was famous for traveling with racing hounds, peacocks, and sleek horses.

When Custer's Seventh Cavalry was ordered out of Fort Abraham Lincoln to the Black Hills to secure the area from reportedly hostile Indians, Mary and Charles stayed behind with Mrs. Custer. After the battle at The Little Big Horn, Mary remained in Bismarck, where she purchased 120 acres as a homestead near Spearfish. There is no verified photograph of Mary Kercherval, although a few "possibles" can be found in South Dokata. Charles and his wife Elizabeth Kercherval raised nine children on the old homestead.

Meanwhile, Beatrice Cotton was born in Oklahoma, descended from French Creole stock, with an Apache grandmother, who was born a slave. Like others of the time, the grandmother and her young charges migrated north and westward as soon after emancipation as possible. Beatrice married Roland Kercherval, a son of Charles and Elizabeth Kercheval.

The story of Beatrice's and Roland's courtship is a familiar one, given the times. Beatrice's father required that she wait until she was twenty-one

6. Among the black women who worked as cooks and maids for the Custers, perhaps the best known is "Aunt Sally" Campbell, who is buried at Galena, South Dakota.

Roland and Beatrice Kercherval, circa 1910, in Edgemont, South Dakota. (Courtesy of Beatrice Kercherval, Edgemont)

to marry her handsome suitor. After a long and arduous courtship, the two married and lived in a succession of towns in the eastern Wyoming/western South Dakota area, where they farmed and raised cattle, grain, turkeys, and hay. Beatrice worked occasionally in Sheridan, Wyoming, and Buffalo, South Dakota.

BASS REEVES

The term "hero" hangs well on the broad shoulders of Bass Reeves. For his time, he was a sizable man: six feet, two inches tall, weighing 200 pounds, he proudly wore a deputy marshall's badge, pinned to his breast pocket by "hanging judge" Isaac C. Parker in the Oklahoma Territory of 1875.

Born a slave near Paris, Lamar County, Texas, in 1824, Reeves developed a notable proficiency as a fistfighter and wrestler. In his thirties, he got into an argument with his master, knocked him out and fled northward across the Red River into free territory. There, he formed close relationships with Seminole and Creek Indians, even fighting in Civil War battles for them.

Although he could neither read nor write, Reeves was noticed by Judge Parker, who deputized other marshals "of color" like Zeke Miller, Bud Ledbetter, and Grant Johnson (half Indian, half black, called the "mulatto from Eufaula") to deal with increasing crimes committed by newly freed black men and unruly white settlers who had begun to flock to the territory in search of cheap land.

Accidentally supportive of the judge's work, the Indians known as the Five Civilized Tribes had once kept slaves themselves; they were thus at ease around black men and women, tending to trust them more than the intrusive whites. Parker recognized this connection as fortuitous and appointed several African Americans to the job. Reeves was the first black he deputized.

Bass Reeves, lawman. (Courtesy of the Coe Library, Reference Department, University of Wyoming, Laramie)

Deputy U.S. marshalls of Judge Isaac C. Parker, Oklahoma Territory. At the same time that Bass Reeves was sworn in, so were (left to right): Amos Maytubby, Zeke Miller, Neely Factor, and Bob L. Fortune. (Courtesy of the Denver Public Library, Western History Collection, Colorado)

Reeves was noted for his style as a lawman: he used disguises and pretense to catch criminals.[7] At times, he worked out an arrangement with a number of Indians in order to collect several criminals before heading back with them to Judge Parker's courtroom. That way, he could spend more time hunting down lawbreakers.

Known for his guile and inventiveness in the tracking of badmen (reportedly credited with handcuffing a group of seven outlaws while they slept), Reeves became famous for his extraordinary successes as a lawman. He was equally legendary for his ambidextrous skill with pistols, excellent riding abilities, and his convincing use of aliases.

In his career as a lawman, Reeves arrested over three thousand lawbreakers, collecting the rewards on many of them.

7. During the 1930s, Reeves achieved a degree of national fame in magazine articles and newspapers published on the east coast. Also during this time, a young radio writer, Fran Stryker, was searching for a character he could create who would appeal to listeners of popular radio programs. Although no documentation exists to prove that Stryker wrote into his scripts a figure modeled on this black lawman who worked in Texas and Oklahoma—a figure who displayed great skill at storytelling, disguises, riding, and shooting; a figure who wore a mask and also rode with an Indian companion—could Bass Reeves be the prototype for one of the most famous western radio characters of all time: the Lone Ranger?

The Shores family of western Nebraska was one of the first to settle in this flat and dry part of the West. (Courtesy of the Nebraska State Historical Society, Lincoln)

Homesteaders in Nebraska

The sides of the trail were lined with negroes, headed for Topeka and Emporia, Kansas to get a free farm and a span of mules from the State Government. Over my pack there was a large buffalo robe, and on my saddle hung a fine silver- mounted Winchester rifle. These attracted the attention of those green cotton-field negroes, who wore me out asking questions about them. Some of these negroes were afoot, while others drove donkeys and oxen.

(Charles Siringo [1927, 101], describing what he witnessed in 1879)

Most wagon trains heading west were composed solely of whites. It was less a matter of racism (although it probably was an issue) than one of economics. The trail west was arduous, long, and expensive. To purchase a heavy-duty wagon (the trusty Conestoga, for example), clothing fit for the journey and the destination, food for three to seven months' travel, horses, and mules and to pay a share of the guides' expenses, and so forth, the costs could amount to the modern equivalent of $30,000 or more. Not many ex-slaves had that level of resources.

Understandably, their newly gained freedom fed their wish to journey westward to new lands. Banding together without experienced guides, and with minimal equipment, they found their way by following the wheel ruts of those who had preceded them. Their journey took them across Kansas and Iowa and on to the Dakotas and Nebraska.

The Chadron, Nebraska, Photographs

Photographs are easy prey to damage and deterioration from any number of sources. The Chadron photographs suffered the ravages of time, but now have been given a relatively safe haven in the library archives at Chadron State University.

Near the turn of the century, R. W. Graves set up his photo parlor in Chadron. He began recording and preserving images relating to his life and business: local town citizens, Indians, scenic views of the Plains and bluffs of northern Nebraska, and a rare, black doll baby—obviously the pride of some child. Over eleven hundred glass plates, tintypes, and negatives have survived and remain in the collection.

Earliest known photograph of African Americans in the Nebraska Territory, 1865. (Photograph by C. W. Walker; courtesy of the Nebraska State Historical Society, Lincoln)

Like most small towns in the West, Chadron was home to African Americans, some of them, as is apparent in the photographs, achieving a relatively high level of income and acceptance into the community. The photographs of Chadron's black citizens are few in number, reflecting the low population percentage. The poor physical condition of the photographs reproduced here illustrates the ephemeral nature of photography. Because of poor storage facilities, water damage, and other factors too varied to calculate prior to residence in the library archives, this evidence of the African American experience in the American West was nearly lost.

The Chadron, Nebraska, photographs are reproduced courtesy of the R. W. Graves Collection, Chadron State University Library. All of the individuals in the photographs are unidentified.

CHAPTER TEN

DESERT AND MOUNTAINS
Arizona, Utah, Nevada

Arizona

In the Kansas and Oklahoma territories there was the influx of African Americans who became farmers, sheepherders, and cattlemen; in the arid Southwest there was another hardy group of emigrants who braved the rigors of dry desert, high mountains, and belligerent Indians. Foremost among them were the Southwestern military and their scouts, but there were also black families who helped settle the area and whose descendants remain.

FORT VERDE, ARIZONA

Buffalo soldiers were assigned to Fort Verde (built in 1871 as Camp Verde) in central Arizona to protect settlers who had begun farming along the

(left) Mrs. Charles Soper, circa 1870, is photographed in her role of nursemaid to a white child, one of the most common employment opportunities for African American women in the early West. (Courtesy of the Sharlott Hall Museum, Prescott, Arizona)

(top left) A black soldier and three Navajo scouts who worked out of Fort Verde, Arizona, and probably Forts Wingate and Whipple. Military men were usually assigned to groups of scouts when on duty because of the hostile environment during the Indian wars. This style of studio portrait was popular; it was usually sent home to the family as a remembrance. (Courtesy of the Fort Verde State Park, Arizona)

(bottom left) Inside the guardhouse at San Carlos, Arizona. The man on the right, a trooper in the Ninth Cavalry, is wearing his "field dress," which was regulation since the heavy woolen military uniform was impractical in Arizona's climate. (Courtesy of the Sharlott Hall Museum, Prescott, Arizona)

(above left) A *carte-de-visite* of Nancy Simpson from Prescott, Arizona, on the back of which is written, "This is one of the girl's sayings, 'Well, I must go home pretty soon. In fact, sooner than that. Will be back right away.' Miss Nancy Simpson now Mrs. Richardson February 23, 1868. Nancy Simpson who worked 3 1/2 years for us in Junction, Arizona." (Courtesy of the Sharlott Hall Museum, Prescott, Arizona)

(above right) "Renegade Negro" photograph by Wittick Studios, circa 1883. No history of this photo exists. AWOL troopers were not uncommon given the rugged life and long periods of boredom for young men whose sense of adventure led them to seek another way of life. Desertion rates often exceeded 50 percent, and military divisions were seldom, if ever, at full strength. Note the fake background of this studio portrait, a common practice of early photographers, who often supplied the subject with inaccurate dress and firearms. The object was to promote selling the photographs to primarily eastern customers. (Courtesy of the Arizona Historical Society, Phoenix)

These snapshots of the world's most famous black cowboy entertainer were probably taken by a young Barry Goldwater; Bill Pickett is performing his trademark bulldogging feat in which he bit the bull's lip, forcing the animal to its knees. (Courtesy of the Barry Goldwater Collection, Arizona Historical Foundation, Tempe)

Black troopers with water wagon. (Courtesy of the Fort Verde State Park, Ft. Verde, Arizona)

Verde River and West Clear Creek. The black troopers stationed at Camp Verde, at various times, were from the Ninth and Tenth Cavalries and the Twenty-Fourth Infantry. Their duty assignments included protecting U.S. interests in much of the southwestern United States. At one time they were commanded by Gen. George Crook, who survived the battle of the Little Big Horn in Montana and fought the last major battle with the Chiricahua Apaches in 1882. The battle at Big Dry Wash was one of the bloodiest of its time and seemed to have ended the armed rebellions of the Apaches.

The presence of women was rare but not unusual in military life. Black as well as white women were often hired as laundrywomen (as Emma Wright

African American troopers and white officers preparing to ride into the Arizona high country, circa 1890. (Courtesy of the Fort Verde State Park, Arizona)

may have been), an occupation that let them be close to their husbands, lovers, or sons. At other times, they might also be cooks, or prostitutes, or nurses, or nannies to white children. In short, women were hired and encouraged to support the mission of their men.

Life on a military reservation was not always concerned with deadly struggles and battles with Indians; there were periods when an ordinary life-style, concerned with issues of daily existence, was possible. The presence of children was not uncommon, and all of them shared in the daily experiences of the young. There are no indications of racial discrimination toward black children, who seemed to be treated well.

Fort Verde was midway between Forts Apache and Whipple, both about a two day's ride, one to the east and the other to the west. Children often attended school at Fort Whipple or were boarded in Prescott to avoid duplicating efforts at the smaller installations.

THE JOHN SLAUGHTER RANCH, ARIZONA

As mentioned ealier, Cabeza de Vaca's expedition of 1540–41 brought with it one of the most intriguing characters in western history: Estevan,

Mrs. Emma Wright (Knight?), circa 1880, wearing a quasi-military dress she undoubtedly fashioned herself. Since there were no women in the military at this time, she may have selected the dress in acknowledgment of her husband, who was probably serving at Fort Smith, Arkansas. (From author's collection)

(top) Summer camp at Fern Springs, August 21, 1887. Summer camps in the high country around Fort Verde were a welcome relief from the heat in lower elevations. Black nursemaids tending their small charges was a common sight. (Courtesy of the National Archives, Washington, D.C.)

(bottom) School children in Prescott, Arizona, circa 1890s, at a time when youngsters from nearby forts began to attend public schools in the area. (From author's collection)

Elderly John Slaughter and family, circa 1900, with the man called "Old Bat" near rear center. (Courtesy of the John Slaughter State Park, Arizona)

the blackamoor. He was a valued, multilingual aide to the famous explorer, and, in a strange turn of fate, was one of the first "Europeans" seen by the Indians in that part of the country.

The mountain passes (Guadalupe or Cottonwood) through which the Cabeza de Vaca expedition—and other "conquerors" as well— most likely moved are along the Mexico/Arizona border near today's Douglas, Arizona. The area is dry, gullied, and crumpled, and in 1882 became part of a 74,000-acre ranch belonging to John Slaughter. The ranch originally spread across two countries and covered hundreds of square miles. Slaughter obtained the land by leasing it from heirs of Ignacio Perez. In 1822, Perez, a Spanish lieutenant, had paid thirty pesos for a grant to the land shortly after Mexico claimed sovereignty from Maximilian and his Spanish lords. Perez had built his hacienda on top of a presidio erected by the Spanish in the 1700s.

In 1830, the Apaches, acting as they had earlier with the Spanish, drove Perez off his land, forcing him to leave his cattle herds behind. Eighteen years later, when Brigham Young's Mormon Battalion swept into the area, along with scout Kit Carson, they found remnants of the Perez cattle—

(top) Estevan as depicted in a nineteenth-century allegorical painting of Spanish troops and an American Indian. (Courtesy of the Tuskegee University Archives, Tuskegee, Alabama)

(bottom) Riders from the Slaughter ranch, which had a contract with the U.S. government to maintain the Mexico/U.S. border in that area. (Courtesy of the John Slaughter State Park, Arizona)

(left) Henry Ossian Flipper, circa 1876, first African American graduate of West Point, was later drummed out of the cavalry on trumped-up charges. He migrated to Slaughter's ranch, where he worked as an engineer. (Courtesy of the John Slaughter State Park, Arizona)

(right) "Old Bat," who lived most of his life with John Slaughter both on the ranch and when Slaughter was sheriff of Tombstone, Arizona. (Courtesy of the John Slaughter State Park, Arizona).

Samuel D. and Amanda L. Chambers, early Latter-day Saints in Utah. (Courtesy of the Church of Jesus Christ of Latter-day Saints, Historical Department, Salt Lake City, Utah)

animals that had survived on the abundant water and forage in the area. Without this fresh meat, by the way, the battalion's journey to San Diego would have been far more difficult that it was.

Two years after Slaughter leased the ranch land, he bought it outright and began to make improvements. Slaughter was also sheriff of Tombstone, Arizona, during that period, and finished his tour in office before moving to the ranch.

The ranch was held by his family until 1936, when it was divided into its "Mexican" property, which was returned to Mexico) and its "U.S." property, which exists today in a much smaller version in the southern part of Arizona. The Nature Conservancy and the U.S. Fish and Wildlife Service operate the historic ranch as representing an important era in this nation's western history.

The John Slaughter ranch operated on a unique social basis: individuals of different racial heritages working and living together.

Utah

The Church of Jesus Christ of Latter-day Saints (or Mormon church) has a checkered history in dealing with racial issues, especially in the twentieth century. A tenet of the church held that black skin was akin to the Biblical mark of Cain. Consequently, there were few African American members of the church in its early history. There were some black Mormons, however, and they led high-profile existences, given the times, place, theology, and politics.

The area was known to non-Mormons as well as Mormons. In the 1800s there were black adventurers, explorers, and cowboys who traveled through the region: James Beckworth trapped in the Cache Valley; Isom Dart cowboyed with Butch Cassidy and the Sundance Kid in the area called "Brown's Hole," encompassing parts of Colorado, Wyoming, and Utah; and Jacob Dodson accompanied John Frémont's expeditions in the 1840s. Frederick Sion (a "mulatto") journeyed from England to join this new religious order in the West. Black cowboys like Albert "Speck" Williams, Nat Love, and Deadwood Dick (who spent his last years as a Pullman porter based in Salt Lake City) lived and worked in the territory.

When the Mormons left Illinois in 1847 to find and settle in what they called "Zion," or "The Promised Land," a few black men and women were part of the entourage.

According to legend (and based somewhat on facts), Green Flake drove the wagon in which Brigham Young lay ailing during the trip through the pass above the valley with its salty lake. Whether the story is true or not, ex-slaves Flake, Hark Lay, and Oscar Crosby were with that emigrant wagon train making its historic way into the valley. Flake was probably not a member of the Mormon church, but rather a friend and entrepreneur who ferried the emigrants from Nauvoo, Illinois, to their new homeland.

Green Flake, an early black pioneer in Utah Territory. (Courtesy of the Church of Jesus Christ of Latter-day Saints, Historical Department, Salt Lake City, Utah)

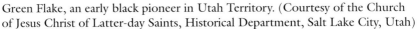

By the mid-1800s both freedmen and indentured slaves were living in the territory. History took a step backwards when the Utah Territorial legislature recognized slavery and indentured bondage as legal institutions, most likely because many influential Mormons had emigrated from the South and brought their slaves with them.

The African Americans who joined the new church were probably less concerned about theological issues and more cognizant that these white pioneers had fled from religious and social oppression that was much like their own oppression by slavery. Besides, white Mormons needed all the help they could get, it seems, in establishing a new life-way in a semiarrid environment.

Prominent black families listed in the church's history included Franklin Perkins, born in 1813; George Stevens; and George Bankhead, the son of a

The caption for these photographs is "Taken at Utah Pioneer Jubilee, Salt Lake City, July 24, 1894." The group, "Utah Pioneers of 1847," includes the African American woman in the lower picture. (Courtesy of the Church of Jesus Christ of Latter-day Saints, Historical Department, Salt Lake City, Utah)

white slave-master. Bankhead converted to the Mormon church and moved with his sons to Draper, Utah, in 1852. His brother, John Bankhead, located in the Cache Valley region. Elijah Abel, who attained a high position in the church in Nauvoo as a member of the Quorum of the Seventy, moved his family to "Zion" and helped build the Mormon temple in Salt Lake City. Isaac and Jane James, along with their children, arrived in the Salt Lake Valley in 1847 and lived in and worked for the household of Joseph Smith, the founder of the religion. Smith had been murdered in 1844 in Illinois.

By taking into account the men in the Ninth and Tenth Cavalries stationed at Fort Duchesne and those in the Twenty-Fourth Infantry at Fort Douglas and hundreds of others, including the women and children who were there as well, it becomes apparent that Utah was home to a sizable number of African-Americans in those early years.

The experiences of African Americans in Utah were not unlike those elsewhere in the country: Lynchings occurred. Discrimination in housing accommodations was common, particularly in small, isolated communities governed by strict, conventional Mormons who were unable socially to accept people with black skin except for meeting the most rudimentary needs of physical labor and servitude. The practice of slavery endured until the territory became a state, and had been a major deterrent to Congress's ratification of the petition. Legalized discrimination in the use of public facilities existed until the 1960s in many towns. Despite the negative aspects, black pioneers have added a rich component to life in Utah from the first days of emigration and settlement.

Nevada

In the migration of settlers from the east that swept past the Rocky Mountains into the arid western deserts, there was little tarrying along the way until it reached coastal lands. There were fewer African Americans settling in Nevada—in Utah and northern New Mexico as well—than in other western territories. In 1860, for example, census records indicate fewer than 50 black men and women as residents; forty years later, the number was 134.

Unexpectedly, Nevada was the first state in the nation to ratify the Fifteenth Amendment to the U.S. Constitution, giving African American citizens the vote.

In early 1853, near Genoa (then part of Utah Territory), a young drover,

These Nevada workers in a mineral mine are of different racial backgrounds, circa 1890. (Courtesy of the National Archives, Washington, D.C.)

Ben Palmer, established a ranching operation in conjunction with his sister Charlotte. The sister was married to D. H. Barber, a white man; the families ranched on adjoining acreage in Carson Valley. In 1853, a child, Benjamin Barber, was born to the couple. This event might seem quite ordinary without knowing that the first white child was not born until 1854.

By 1860, black families in the area operated three ranches; Winfield and Sophia Miller worked other ranches. Nevada had refused the vote to African Americans from its first days of statehood, so the general cultural environment was less than congenial. However, the success of the ranching

Ben Palmer, first black rancher in Nevada Territory, circa 1855. With him is Mary Hawkins, a local resident. (Courtesy of the University of Nevada, Reno)

An Eminent African Traveler

Probably the man who has crossed the American continent the greatest number of times is Captain Moses Freeman, the colored commodore of the land craft which transports the big railway officials back and forth. The commodore is in command of the directors' car of the Central Pacific, and it is his duty to convey his superiors to and from about the country. The commodore some six weeks ago took Governor Stanford to New York. Then he came back "empty" and took general superintendent Towne and party to Boston. Tomorrow or day after he starts for New York "empty" to bring out Mr. C.C. Huntington who is coming to attend the directors' meeting in August. "By de time I git him out here," said Captain Freeman yesterday, "de governor will be back from Europe, and I'll have to go and fetch him over." Captain Freeman says he has now crossed the continent one hundred and seventy-eight times.

(From Railroad Age, August 4, 1881; dialect in original)

operations was a catalyst for a change to a more pluralistic society. These new ranchers employed a multiracial crew of Indian, black, and white ranch hands.

As in virtually every other western state in which railroad companies laid track, jobs associated with trains were highly prized since the prospect of permanent employment was greater than with few other occupations in the West. As mentioned earlier, the "front end" jobs (engineers and firemen) were snapped up by white workers as the dominant ethnic group, and the less "desirable" positions (car attendants, cooks, gandy dancers, and conductors) were left to others.

CHAPTER ELEVEN

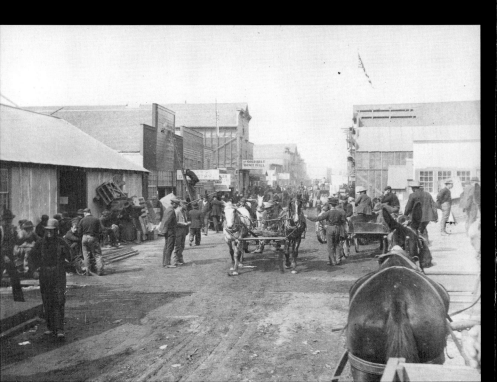

> Already Alaska beckons on the north, and pointing
> to her wealth of natural resources asks the nation on
> what new terms the new age will deal with her.
>
> (Turner [1929] 1986, 120)

POINTS NORTH
Alaska, the Pacific Northwest

Alaska

African Americans were drawn northward during the gold rush years and the era of great whaling ships along with other adventurers of every racial heritage. It was the middle of the nineteenth century, and the tales of riches to the north attracted a multitude of people to some of the most forbidding land and seas on earth. Those spreading across Alaska were miners, gamblers, trappers, freight haulers, whalers, whores, businessmen and women, cooks, and soldiers, to name a few.

Prostitutes, called "creoles" because of their mixed Russian and Indian genes, apparently accompanied the first American troops to occupy the land in 1867. Although not listed as residents by any legal documents, • these women most likely plied their trade and washed clothes for the military, the latter occupation a common one for poor women, camp followers, and wives of enlisted men.

(left) Nome, Alaska, during the gold rush. Miners from all over the world collected on the streets. Note the unidentified African American on the left in the picture. (Courtesy of the Anchorage Museum of History and Art, Alaska)

In 1880, a census of primarily southern Alaska found no African Americans to report. Most likely, Canadians were the early migrants to the Northwest Territories and "Seward's Folly," as Alaska was often called. The first known African American to be on an official list was James Walker in Sitka in October 1870. He was noted as "male, Negro, aged 25" (Sackinger 1975:3). Apparently born in Panama, Walker worked as a cook and was married to Maria, a woman whose racial background was not listed, but who had been born in Sitka.

By 1890, records indicate that 112 persons of "color" resided in the territory, variously listed as "negroes, mulattoes, Hawaiians, Malays, and Portuguese mulattoes from the Cape Verde Islands." Apparently, all of them were in the whaling business, and lived in places as remote and disparate as Cape Smythe, Point Barrow, and Port Clarence. As one researcher wrote: "Blacks were among the thousands of people who flocked to the Klondike gold fields" (Overstreet 1990:17).

WHALING

The days of great whaling ships began with hearty adventurers and businessmen out of New Bedford, Massachusetts, and other whaling ports on the east coast of the United States. Primarily sailing the Atlantic, Pacific, and Indian Oceans hunting the gigantic beasts, these mariners spent upwards of eight months at a time at sea, returning only when weather or overloaded holds forced a return to home port for a respite of a few weeks. In Alaska, however, the whaling procedure was different. Since crews spent several months sailing from the east coast to their destinations on the northwestern coast, there was little profit in sailing all the way back round the tip of South America to return home; sound economics would not allow that much nonproductive time at sea. Instead, crews stayed over the winter months in safe harbors like those near Barrow and Hope on the northern coast, sailing only halfway south to transfer their loads. By staying as late as possible prior to the onset of winter, crews could harvest a large number of whales. The trick was to avoid staying too long, however, and being trapped by the rapidly forming ice floes that could destroy both men and ships. Often they judged poorly and were trapped.

Arguably the most well-known captain of any U.S. revenue cutter was Michael "Mad Mike" Healy, a black man who sailed the *Bear* in Alaskan waters for several years. He was a controversial figure in many ways. Healy had light skin, which, given the times, probably allowed his rise to the rank of captain. Although skilled and proficient in his trade, he was also pos-

(top) U.S. revenue cutter, the *Bear*. Its most famous captain was Michael Healy, an African American whose deeds are well remembered in the sailing history of that region. The ship plied Alaskan waters during the 1880s. (From author's collection)

(bottom) "Mad Mike" Healy, captain of the *Bear* (on the right) with his crew. He commanded the ship from 1886 to 1896. Not as well recorded were his shorter commands of the ships *McCullock* (1900) and *Thelis* (1902–1903). (Courtesy of the Rasmussen Collection, University of Alaska Archives, Fairbanks)

Whaling crew, Alaska, circa 1890. Men came from New England, Europe, the Cape Verde Islands, Tonga, Samoa, and elsewhere for work on whaling ships in the Pacific Ocean and Bering Straits. (Courtesy of the Rasmussen Collection, University of Alaska Archives, Fairbanks)

sessed of a violent temper and a penchant for mistreating his crew. He was brought up on charges more than once for poor leadership, but his "connections" (a brother-in-law in Washington, D.C., allegedly was influential in sustaining Healy's rank and tenure) apparently protected him from punishment. Under his captaincy, the *Bear* became one of the best known revenue cutters of its time, and was the most photographed of any other such ship. And of the men under his command: many were African American.

Not all dark-skinned crewmen were from New England; many were from the South Sea islands, as was Queequeg, one of Herman Melville's main characters in *Moby Dick*.[1] At first, the New Englanders were few in number

1. Along with Arabic names such as Ishmael (the narrator in the novel), Melville loaded his writing of *Moby Dick* with guarded references to black seamen. The name of the ship, *Pequod*, seems to be an indirect reference to the Pequot Mashintucket ("black") Indians of New England. Concepts of "black" and "white" were clearly on Melville's mind.

on board the whaling ships; eventually, over the years, they were in the majority.

Other crew members from the United States and Jamaica listed in early head counts were probably forerunners of the northward migration from English and French possessions in the West Indies that would occur in the early twentieth century.

GOLD MINERS

The year 1890 began a most auspicious time for Alaska: the gold rush decade. With the discovery of gold in the Klondike, thousands of men (and the inevitable camp followers) poured northward into a most inhospitable region for working in the outdoors year-round.

As many as 100,000 men came by sled, carriage, horse, and foot up from Washington and Idaho through British Columbia or sailed by ship up the Inland Passage out of Seattle to trailheads in Sitka, Nome, Dawson, Ketchikan, and Skagway.

An African American crew of a whaling ship, lined up for an informal portrait. By the time the American whaling trade ended, over 90 percent of the crews were African American. (Courtesy of the Providence Public Library Archives, Rhode Island)

Miners at the base of Chilkoot Pass, waiting their turn for the twenty-mile climb into the northern regions of the territory. Note African American man (hands on hips), center left. (Courtesy of the Alaska State Archives, Juneau)

Black miner on a street in Nome, Alaska, circa 1890. (Courtesy of the National Park Service, Anchorage, Alaska)

OTHER ALASKAN ADVENTURERS

Black federal troops of Company L, Twenty-Fourth Infantry, were stationed at Skagway and Fort Wrangell (later, at Fort Saint Michael, Fort Gibbon, Fort Egbert, Fort David, Fort Liscum, and Circle) to keep order amid the fervor of the gold rush. Posted at the beginning of the twenty-mile climb over Chilkoot Pass, for example, the infantry kept a semblance of law even in this remote spot.

Dawson was typical of most towns in many ways. The population consisted of 75 percent Americans, 10 percent Canadians, and a smattering of individuals of other nationalities with various racial backgrounds. It became a boomtown in the late 1890s. One black man, St. John Atherton,

The Twenty-Fourth Infantry at Skagway. The soldiers were stationed at several places in the territory more to protect miners from each other than the general populace during the entire period of the gold rush. (Courtesy of the National Park Service, Anchorage, Alaska)

sluiced gold worth $30,000 in the spring of that year. Born a slave near Atlanta, he expressed a desire to return to the plantation, buy it, and return it as a gift to its original owner's daughter. It is not known if he actually carried out his wish.

Other Dawson characters were The Black Prince, a prizefighter; Arthur Jordan, an ex-slave and cook who became a well-known man-about-town; Mrs. Mason, a laundrywoman who made a small fortune serving miners' needs—and lost it to Soapy Smith, an infamous white con man from Denver, Colorado, who had moved north where the pickings were richer.

Other black pioneering trailblazers who turned Seward's Folly into a dynamic place to live were Black Alice, who made her fortune in Nome selling dinners for $5.00—the equivalent of $150 per dinner order in today's money; Leonard Seppala, who raced his dogsleds near Nome; and Black Kitty, who practiced the world's oldest profession in the Klondike.

Washington and Oregon

Records of black pioneers in the Northwest date from the late 1700s when traders recognized the value of the area's fur-bearing game. Marcus Lopez, a Cape Verdian who was a crewman on Captain Robert Gray's *Lady Washington* (sailed from Boston to the northwest coast in 1787 to load furs), became the first African American to step onto the shores of the Pacific Northwest. York, the African American who was with the Lewis and Clark expedition arrived on the coast approximately fifteen years later.

With slavery still practiced in the South, there were few black settlers who found their way into this part of the country. By the mid-1800s, however, a few more had followed the tracks of the Oregon Trail northwestward. After seven months on the trail, George Bush and a few hardy colleagues found their way to The Dalles, south of the Columbia River

Bush, a freeman in his native Pennsylvania, became the community's leader. A successful farmer, he also purchased a ship, the *Orbit*, and became a trader in lumber in west coast ports. Unfortunately, he died prior to the passage of the Thirteenth and Fourteen Admendments to the Constitu-

Sketch of George Bush. (Courtesy of Ralph Hayes, Seattle, Washington)

Canyon City, Oregon, circa 1860. When gold rush fever spread northward from California, rugged miners moved with it. These two men prospected around Canyon City in the mid-1860s. (Courtesy of the Grant City Museum, Canyon City)

tion, giving citizenship rights to African Americans, so he never legally became a "full and complete" citizen.

His son, William Owen Bush, became a progressive and nationally known farmer who was elected to Washington State's initial legislature which established the state's first college of agriculture, later to become Washington State University at Pullman.

George Washington was born a slave in Virginia in 1817, but, like his namesake, George Washington Bush, he migrated westward along the Oregon Trail as a freeman. Prior to his move west, Washington took his considerable size and strength into the forest, where he was, at various times, sawmill operator, weaver, tanner, cook, and moonshiner. After moving to Washington and marrying Mary Jane Cooness, a Jewish black woman

(top left) George Washington, circa 1870. (Courtesy of the Oregon Historical Society, Portland)

(bottom left and right) George Washington and his first wife Mary Jane Cooness. (Courtesy of the Lewis County Historical Museum, Chehalis, Washington)

from Portland, Washington settled his family near the Chehalis River. It was a most propitious decision.

In 1872 he heard that the Northern Pacific Railroad was going to build a roadway across that part of the state. Seizing the initiative, Washington platted a town, Centerville, and started advertising the lots he had set aside for sale. The town was renamed Centralia, and became prosperous, surviving the Panic of 1873 when Washington used his own money to provide food for the community and help it change from a logging industry to a more diversified economy.

ROSLYN, WASHINGTON: A CASE STUDY

Tucked away in forested mountains one hundred miles east of Seattle is the small community of Roslyn, noted more today for its verdant beauty and location sites for movies and television programs than its connection to black western history.

Founded as a coal mining town by the Oregon-Washington Improvement Company, it had been a white community from its beginnings until the day miners decided to strike for improved wages and working conditions in 1888. The so-called Northern Pacific coal strike was responsible for several deaths and, quite unintentionally, a radical change in the ethnography of the area.

The coal company decided not to negotiate with striking miners. Instead, recruiters fanned out across the southern states to locate black men willing to move to and work in the far reaches of the Pacific Northwest. Many young men jumped at the chance to find employment in new and attractive surroundings, and some brought wives and families with them.

It was not until they were actually en route, in coach cars, that most were told they were going to be strikebreakers. Whatever their reaction was to that announcement is not known, but most of the men stayed on the train and relocated in Roslyn. Once there, they were met with catcalls and racial slurs. Yet, they persevered. Over the period of a decade, Roslyn would become a predominantly black community.

Lucy Breckenridge and her son John arrived in Roslyn with the strike-

(top right) Lucille and John Breckenridge, Roslyn, Washington, circa 1898. (Courtesy of the Spokane Northwest Black Pioneers, Washington State)

(bottom right) Spokane's first African American police officer, Henry W. Sample, who served from 1892 to 1895, with his favorite horse. (Courtesy of the Spokane Public Library, Washington State)

breakers in 1888. Accompanying Lucy from Virginia were her husband Henry and Mary Perkins, Henry's sister.

African American families, like the Donaldsons, Smalleys, Clarks, Ammon-nettes (all of whom came to Roslyn during its mining days) and others whose names are lost to history were the foundation of a thriving community that lasted until the 1930s.

Idaho

Most of the loggers, miners, farmers, military personnel, and cowboys who arrived in the Northwest in the late 1800s did not stay. Those who did turned to homesteading and the raising of families. In 1855, for example, Seattle had approximately fifty residents who were not American Indians; Oregon had a similarly small number of African Americans.

Among the African American pioneers in the Idaho region were Joe and Lou Wells. Joe, born a slave in 1858 in North Carolina, took the surname

Big-timber loggers worked in the virgin forests of Idaho in the late 1800s. Joe, Roy, and Chuck Wells, along with an unidentified white man, are the lumberjacks in this picture. (Courtesy of the Latah County Historical Society, Moscow)

Joe and Lou Wells, circa 1888. (Courtesy of the Latah County Historical Society, Moscow, Idaho)

of the Wells brothers Frank and Crom in 1889 when he and his wife migrated to Idaho. They lived near Pine Creek, in the vicinity of Moscow, where Joe was a successful blacksmith. He liked to joke that "I am the only white man in the Spud Hill area . . . the rest are all Swedes."

The range of African American pioneering in what demographers often call the "empty quarter" of the United States was as varied as anywhere else, but the number of pioneers was fewer than elsewhere. Still, individuals and families who moved there in the late 1800s and early 1900s formed the basis of today's thriving populations.

CHAPTER TWELVE

"HAOLE 'ELE 'ELE"
IN OWHYEE

Geographically, the Sandwich Islands were far distant from the western shores of the United States, even in the days of sailing ships. However, economics, political interests, changing population patterns, and a growing sea trade reduced the 2,600 miles of open water to a manageable barrier for both black and white entrepreneurs.[1]

By the time the British sailing captain James Cook landed his expedition on the beaches of Oahu in 1778, other nations were also extending their spheres of influence throughout this part of the world. Stories about Cook's exploits filtered back to the European continent and were the apparent source of

1. The Polynesian term haoli 'ele 'ele translates as "foreign black," which was the closest native Hawaiians could come to describing the dark-skinned men and women who began to move to their islands in the early nineteenth century.

(left) Whaling in the South Seas. This segment of an oil-on-canvas painting was probably done by a crewman. It shows a whaling boat from the good ship Uncas on its initial trip to the Sandwich Islands, circa 1868. The racial diversity of the crew is obvious. (From author's collection)

Members of King Kamahameha's naval guard, circa 1900. (Courtesy of the Hawaii State Archives, Honolulu)

avaricious foreign interest in these new and "savage" lands. Nations world-wide sent sailing ships to the islands, and today their crews' descendants are a large segment of the island chain's non-Polynesian population.

The islands (later known as "Owhyhee" and, in the nineteenth century, as "Hawai'i") were magnets for foreigner investors, sailors, businessmen, and missionaries—and they were often African Americans.

The first recorded African American entrepreneur in the Hawaiian Islands was Anthony Allen, a fugitive slave from "German Flats" (probably Schenectady) in New York State, who arrived in Oahu circa 1810 and set up shop near Waikiki Beach. There are no verifiable depictions of Allen (photographers had yet to arrive), but his influence was felt throughout the area. Owner of a bar, a boarding house, and a bowling alley,[2] he also established a neighborhood hospital, started a small truck farm on which he grew vegetables to sell, and ran a "house of entertainment" that catered to sailors.

Allen was a popular figure, and records exist of his meetings with visiting dignitaries and politicians. King Kamehameha the Great, who designated Allen his "trusted advisor," welcomed African American immigrants to his kingdom.[3] In time, Allen married a Hawaiian woman and lived out his years enjoying his island-centered fame until his death circa 1835.

In the early "village years" of the 1840s, Honolulu was home to many African Americans. One such pioneer was Charles H. Nicholson. He was a prosperous tailor, well known for his congeniality, his all-linen suits, and the white adobe building that housed his shop for nearly twenty years (Greer 1977).

Due to the fickleness of history and prejudice, the location of Nicholson's grave is unknown. However, the graves of his wife and son—half Hawaiian, half black—are well marked in Kawaiahao Cemetery. Local lore indicates that because of the color of his skin he was not allowed to be buried in consecrated ground, but his wife and son suffered no such discrimination by the church warden.

Hawai'i's population began to grow dramatically as immigrants arrived, lured by the money inherent in the sea trades of commerce and whaling and in growing sugarcane and pineapple farming, all developed to satisfy the mainland's growing need for food and appetite for foreign goods. Throughout the mid-1800s small shops and service industries blossomed in response to demand and commercial centers developed into cities and towns. In short order, there arrived white missionaries, Chinese and Japanese laborers, Koreans, Bermudans, Filipinos, Polynesians from the outermost reaches of the Pacific Ocean, Portuguese, Puerto Ricans, Jews,

2. "Rolling alleys" were extremely popular in the mid-1800s, especially in Honolulu. Herman Melville, author and seaman, worked for a time as a pinsetter in one of them; whether it was Allen's is not known (Schmitt 1980, 81)

3. Hawai'i is the only "royal kingdom" acquired by the United States, which makes its history beyond the experience of many mainlanders and difficult for them to assess. Various kings and queens of the islands hired black soldiers, sailors, household guards, and musicians throughout their reigns. In 1812, for example, an African American, surnamed Anderson, was court armorer to King Kamehameha's nephew (Porter 1996, 194).

Young Portuguese or Jamaican woman, photographed in Hawai'i, circa 1890. References to Portugal often carried the connotation of "black" in early days since the Cape Verde Islands, lying west of Africa, were a Portuguese colony. For many, she typified the mixed racial heritage of one subgroup of Hawaiian society. (Courtesy of the Bishop Museum, Honolulu)

Mormons, Lutherans, and more, creating one of the most active and polyglot microsocieties in this hemisphere.

Hunting the great whales began for North Americans in the mid-1600s, located primarily on the New England coast. Two hundred years later a huge industry had been built on processing the oil, meat, and hard tissues of these enormous mammals for a wide variety of uses.

Between the 1700s, when the industry was flourishing, and the 1920s, when it all ended, the percentage of black men taking to the sea went from 20 percent to nearly 80 percent, representing men primarily from Portuguese West Africa (Senegal and the Cape Verde Islands, today). An absurd set of circumstances was taking place: in the midst of the American and European slave-trade years, when their kin were being sold into slavery, black Africans were also being avidly recruited as free and equal crewmen for Yankee whalers out of Nantucket, New Bedford, and Mystic (Simpson and Goodman 1986, 79)—a triumph of opportunistic schizophrenia. (Few African American men were recruited for sea duty in those early years, but

Flensing (skinning) a whale as it is loaded on the ship. Whales were "peeled" of their skins, not unlike rolling a log in the water. (Courtesy of the Providence Public Library Archives, Rhode Island)

Statue of a Cape Verde "Big Jim" whaleman—posed for by a sailor—singing and playing his banjo. Statue is at the Lahaina Whaling Museum, Hawaii. (Sculptor: Reems Mitchell; courtesy of the Lahaina Whaling Museum and Rick Ralston)

others[4] were drawn to the trade in numbers that would increase dramatically over time.)

The West African men brought more than their sea legs to the the Atlantic and Pacific Oceans. Tucked in their ditty bags were stringed instruments, later to be called "banjos." This instrument was the perfect musical companion for the Portuguese "squeeze-box" or accordion. The two would become the standard backup for chanteys sung by sailors as they sailed the seven seas.

In 1811 Steven Francis, a cook on the whaling ship New Hazard, jumped ship in Oahu and joined the hundreds of other men who had similarly chosen a new way of life on dry land.[5] Crewmen from ships such as Co-

4. Frederick Douglass spent formative years on the wharves of Baltimore, learning sailing trades, mingling with seamen of varied racial heritage and experience. All of which, he once remarked, added greatly to the convictions that would shape his later life (Trivelli 1995, 100).

5. Jumping ship was not only common but was tacitly encouraged by ships' captains, especially on return voyages when holds were crowded with cargo. Since the crews were not paid until they reached their home port, any "missing" sailor's "parts" (share of the bounty brought home) were kept by the captain or the holding company.

Betsy Stockton arrived in Hawai'i in the early 1800s and began a long career in church service and teaching in the islands and back on the mainland, as well. (Courtesy of the Mission House Museum Library, Honolulu)

lumbia, Santa Rosa, and Argentine were credited by local newspapers for contributing new citizens in 1818. By 1836, at least one ship, the American whaler Chelsea, had lost 10 percent of its crew in one evening. Black crew members such as David Pine, Thomas Johnson, John Wilson, Elyners Case, and Lewis Temple[6] who jumped ship in Hawai'i during the mid-1800s added to the population of an island "paradise," where "all racial groups . . . are minorities" (Nordyke 1988, 241).

During the time Anthony Allen was enjoying prosperity in Honolulu, religious activity was at its peak in all the settlements of the island chain. Missionaries from the Church of Jesus Christ of Latter-day Saints (Mormons) and the Presbyterian church were especially prominent in their religious zeal to convert and save the souls of native islanders. For example, Presbyterian missionary Charles Stewart brought his family to Maui in 1823 and opened the Sandwich Island Mission in Lahaina. Along with him came the nursemaid and household worker Betsy Stockton.

Born a slave to Major Robert Stockton in Princeton, New Jersey,[7] Stockton was described as "precocious and bright." She quickly learned the

6. As inventor of the toggle harpoon, Temple became part of whaling history with his iron lance equipped with a T-shaped head that was designed not to pull free of the whale's body.

7. Many historians note that there were more black slaves in northeastern cities than in all the southern slave states. Prior to emancipation, New York City had a higher population of slaves and indentured servants than in any southern city.

Hawaiian language, which she used in her fiery sermonizing. The Reverend Stewart and all who witnessed her zealous Christianity were impressed (Andrew n.d., 160). In short order she set up a school in Lahaina in which she taught children's classes. Her stay in the islands was relatively short. She left the islands with Stewart when he returned to Cooperstown, New York, in 1825. But her influence continued.

In succeeding years, Stockton led a movement to form the First Presbyterian Church of Colour in Princeton, New Jersey, in 1848. Later she opened a school for black students in Philadelphia (1898) and established a school for Indians in Canada. Her story is singularly important to appreciating the various contributions by African Americans in American history.

Back in the Hawaiian Islands: by the 1840s, black military and royal aides were well-known aspects of Hawaiian society. George H. Hyatt, an African American, as one example for the decade, was appointed leader of the royal band.

Several dozen black missionaries journeyed to the Hawaiian Islands in the nineteenth century (Broussard 1990, 129), but virtually none of them stayed or can be traced to anyone in today's island population.

Carlotta Stewart was a teacher who came to the islands with her father T. McCants Stewart in 1898. McCants Stewart was a freeborn (1852) African American from Charleston, South Carolina, who studied at Howard University prior to graduating with a degree in law in 1875. After working as a journalist in New York City and becoming caught up in the Back to Africa movement, he journeyed to Liberia. He sailed with his daughter to the islands at the end of the century.

Carlotta graduated from Oahu College (Punahou School) with a degree in teaching, a profession she practiced in the islands until 1924. As the principal of a multicultural elementary school, she was well known throughout the islands and became a figure in middle-class Hawaiian society. She lived until 1952.

In 1881 U.S. Secretary of State James G. Blaine led a movement urging African Americans to relocate to the Hawaiian Islands for employment in harvesting crops. At issue was the "unacceptable" presence of Asians (a prejudicial attitude of the times), most of whom were employed as field hands. As part of the "American solution" to the problem, Secretary Blaine had sugar growers and owners of pineapple companies recruit workers from the southern United States. The process was halted when, in 1882, the Hawaiian legislature barred the hiring and importation of African American workers by sugar plantation owners.

In the early 1900s, however, many African Americans came to Oahu

Carlotta Stewart (shown circa 1900) graduated from Hawaiian schools. Her teaching and administrative careers, both in the islands and on the mainland, led to inclusion in Hawaiian society and fame. (Courtesy of the Moorland-Spingarn Research Collection, Howard University, Washington, D.C.)

Pineapple field hands, Hawaiian Islands, circa 1880. This enlargement from a stereograph shows African American workers during the short-lived practice of recruiting men from the southern States. (Courtesy of the Hawaii State Archives, Honolulu)

when the Twenty-Fifth Infantry was relocated to bases near Honolulu. Additional servicemen in the Army, Navy, and other contingents arrived as well.

In 1901 sugar plantations again recruited black field workers from the South—some two hundred from Tennessee. But the plan failed when virtually all of them rebelled and returned to their home state within two years.

With the institution of large-scale farming after the turn of the century and—most important—the establishment of military bases on nearly all of the Hawaiian Islands, African Americans began to constitute a larger and larger group in "paradise."

Antione DeSant, Cape Verde whaleman, ship's captain, frigate pilot, California gold miner, and member of a family whose lives were dedicated to the sea. He often commanded his ships in the waters of the Hawaiian Islands, and subsequently became prosperous and influential in American sailing trades. (Courtesy of the Mystic Seaport Museum, Connecticut)

The black population of the islands at the end of the twentieth century was approximately 18,000, located mainly on Oahu, but spread across the rest of the island chain. This state, with its reputation for opportunities and its exotic climate continues to attract individuals with differing heritages that are often less "acceptable" on the mainland. Here, thousands of miles away in the warm waters of the Pacific, is a place where a mixture of racial heritages is accepted without hesitation.

CHAPTER THIRTEEN

Follow the drinkin' gourd,
For the old man is a-waitin'
For to carry you to freedom,
Follow the drinkin' gourd.
Now the river bank'll make a mighty good road
The dead trees will show you the way
Left foot, peg foot, travelin' on
Follow the drinkin' gourd.

(Lyrics to a traditional song)

FOLLOW THE DRINKIN' GOURD

Most residents of the United States assume that Canada's historical involvement in black issues has been minimal. In a counter assumption, many Canadians think Americans see black pioneers only in warm, southerly climes. As with so many preconceptions about black pioneers, both of these views are incorrent.

In 1619 a Dutchman named Warre sold twenty slaves in Jamestown, Virginia, for the first time. Some of those men and women went north as property of wealthy residents. By the mid-1600s, it is known that black slaves were bought and sold in Quebec; the first recorded slave sale was in 1628, when Oliver la Jeune was purchased.

Matthew Da Costa, a "mulatto," was an early explorer, linguist, and pioneer who had left his home of La Rochelle in Quebec in 1606 to serve as interpreter of Indian languages for Samuel de Champlain ("the father of Canada"). The 1606 Poutrincourt-Champlain expedition explored Nova Scotia, where Da Costa became a founding member of one of Canada's oldest fraternal clubs, the Order of Good Cheer.

(left) "Heading north." A popular lithograph of the Underground Railroad period. (From author's collection)

"Negresses selling mayflowers on the market place" is the title of a woodcut from *Canadian Illustrated News*, May 5, 1872. The early illustrated newspapers were as popular in Canada as were *Harper's Weekly* and *Leslie's Illustrated Newspaper* in the United States. Sketch by W. O. Carlisle. (From author's collection)

By 1685, slavery was legalized in New France under the Code Noir; four years later King Louis XIV was petitioned by the governor general to allow the open practice of slavery. It is important to note that the king was probably a reluctant participant in the event since he was caught in a financial wrangle between settlers who argued that they were at an economic disadvantage because of slavery in New England and the resultant lower production costs for British Colonial goods. Competition from the slave-holding British colonies forced the French king to make his decision.

There was a distinct difference in the "peculiar institution" as practiced north of the border compared to the institution south of the border. Some Canadian history books allege that "slavery rested lightly" on the shoulders of blacks in that country (Bertley 1977, 27). Without a plantation system in a hot, humid climate, the work assigned to Canadian slaves was, apparently, less rigorous generally; they were not subjected to forced labor as were their counterparts to the south. In 1709 "legal" slavery was authorized throughout the Canadian areas called "New France," and by the mid-1700s, nearly 1,000 black individuals had been brought from New England and the West Indies as part of the Canadian slave trade. By 1759 there were 3,604 slaves in New France.

Generally not acknowledged in U.S. history texts is that after both the American Revolution and the War of 1812, over 42,000 black people fled the colonies, not wishing to be disloyal to the British Crown. These men, women, and children sought refuge in southeastern Canadian provinces— Nova Scotia (called "Acadia"; notably Halifax, the destination of the Maroons[1]) and Ontario—where their descendants live to this day. (Other accounts of black men who fought for the British in the American Revolution remain to be examined in both nations.)

The British government offered freedom to colonial slaves in return for their pledges of fealty to the Crown. As a result, some 5,000 left Georgia in 1782 and over 3,000 sailed from South Carolina after the Treaty of Paris (1783) to travel north. Estimates of their number ran as high as 12 percent of the loyalists who left the American colonies for Canada (Bertley 1977, 39).

In 1793, Lt. Gov. Col. John Graves Simcoe began legislating for an end to slavery by introducing a bill to prevent the further importation of slaves into upper Canada and to free the children of slaves living in Canada when they reached the age of twenty-five. To American slaves, the nation to the north became "the promised land." Almost immediately, large numbers of slaves began to head for Canada, following the "drinkin' gourd" of the song—the Big Dipper in the Ursa Major constellation. A line drawn from the two stars at the right end of the Big Dipper's bowl leads north to Polaris, the guiding Polar Star.

Another migration of African Americans occurred after the War of 1812 when 2,000 left for the Maritime Provinces. In addition, "passengers" on the Underground Railroad began to stream up from the southern states to southern and western Canada.

In the 1820s and 1830s American abolitionists and their religious supporters provided a well-organized system of escape routes to Mexico, the Bahamas, and—on the invisible wheels of the Underground Railroad—to

---

1. "Maroon" is a term used to identify the descendants of black slaves who had escaped their Spanish masters prior to the British take-over of Jamaica. They were especially skilled fighters. The term—a corruption of "Cameroon," the homeland of many slaves—has been both an epithet and a mark of distinction at various times in history.

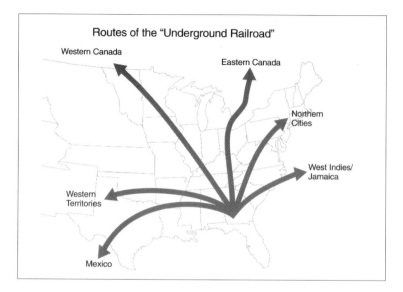

Routes of the "Underground Railroad"

Western Canada

Eastern Canada

Northern Cities

West Indies/ Jamaica

Western Territories

Mexico

Ontario in towns such as Chatham, St. Catherines, Blenheim, Owen Sound, and Amherstberg[2]

Circa 1820, Dan Williams, from the United States, came as a pioneer to western Alberta to work the gold claims and serve as a "cook, trapper, vagrant, idler, or squatter, as chance suited him" (Butler 1915, 216–17). He became friend, co-worker and confidant to early explorers of the Peace River Country in Alberta.

Notable in both black achievements and Canadian history is that Williams sued the Hudson's Bay Company (which was the *de facto* government for much of Canada in those days) over land it had expropriated from him to build a new outpost. Williams protested that his "squatter's rights" superseded those of the company. Williams and gunmen for the Company engaged in a pistol fight, resulting in William's arrest.

In a trial, Williams was found innocent of attempted murder, and his claim to the property was upheld—a rare instance of the Hudson's Bay Company losing a legal case. Williams returned to prospecting and selling

2. In southern Ontario, near the small town of Dresden, Reverend Josiah Henson established a school for runaway slaves. An escaped slave himself, Henson formed a small colony in order to aid and educate the men and women who came to him. In his later years, he was befriended by Harriet Beecher Stowe, who apparently based not only the main character in *Uncle Tom's Cabin* on Henson but also used his stories about slavery as the basis for much of the novel. The small compound is maintained today as a Canadian historic site.

Mines on Dominion Creek in British Columbia, circa 1880. The gold rush lured many Americans northward in the latter half of the nineteenth century. Among them were black men and women; some were slaves, most were free men and women. (Courtesy of the Rasmussem Collection, University of Alaska Archives, Fairbanks)

vegetables to other miners. Never a slave in Canada, Williams was uniquely proud of his new citizen status, often posting signs on his property declaring his loyalty to no one but the Queen of England (Leonard 1995, 140). He died in July 1887 at his cabin.

In August 1833 the practice of slavery was outlawed throughout New France by an act of King William IV of Britain, and Canada became a seductive siren to American slaves. As a means of answering her calls, the Underground Railroad became part of American and Canadian social history. Thousands of sympathetic abolitionists in America and many Canadians participated in the effort; thousands of black men, women, and children found freedom in Ontario and Quebec.

By the 1850s, the black population of Ontario had reached 75,000, amounting to approximately 8 percent of Ontario's total population. And in those same years, the first newspapers for black readers began to be published in Canada.

1873 records indicate that the Cassiar region of British Columbia hosted thousands of prospectors during the gold rush years prior to the richer discoveries in Alaska. Some 300 Chinese and 50 black miners were work-

Honor de Cosmos, born William Smith in Nova Scotia in 1825. This wandering "mulatto" from the California goldfields honed his skills at journalism, oratory, and Freemasonry, rising in political power to defend the union of British Columbia and Vancouver Island, thus bringing British Columbia into the new Canadian confederation. He then served in the second premiership of the province. (Courtesy of the City of Vancouver Archives, B.C.; Out. P. 815, Neg. 373)

ing that area, and one by the name of McDame, struck gold on Dease Creek, B.C. The camp was called "McDame," in his honor.

Another Canadian pioneer of African descent was Col. Stephen Blucke, leader of colonial "black pioneers" who fought for the British in the American Revolution. Along with the Maroons, he left for Nova Scotia, where he became a social leader and entertained Prince William Henry, later King William IV, on his visit to the new land.

John Baker, born a slave in Quebec, fought in many battles in Canada in the 1700s. He joined Wellington's forces at the battle of Waterloo.

Dr. Martin R. Delaney, an explorer and the first black major in the U.S. Army, was a militant who spent most of his life arguing that black men and women needed black leaders. He was also known as one of the first black nationalists. As many others did, Delaney left the States in 1856 and moved to Chatham, Ontario, near the northern terminus of the Underground Railroad in Canada.

Medical men of African descent who fought in the Civil War include Drs. Anderson Rufin Abbott and Alexander T. Augusta. Abbott was born in Toronto in 1837, studied medicine at the University of Toronto and later served as a surgeon in the Union army. Augusta was born in Virginia, later to become Canada's first noted doctor. He studied medicine at Trinity College, University of Toronto. He also served in the Civil War as a major in the cavalry and as a surgeon to the Seventh U.S. Colored Troops. He left the service as a lieutenant colonel.

James Douglas went to Canada as a young man and was an employee of the Hudson's Bay Company, later appointed governor of the British Columbia colony. Born in Demerara, British Guiana, to "Miss Ritchie," a

Victoria pioneer rifle corps ("African Rifles"), an all-black defense force, the first in British Columbia, formed by Gov. James Douglas and the Hudson's Bay Company in 1860. The unit acted as a defense against incursions by the French and invasions by the Americans, who were widely thought to be planning an armed take-over of western Canada. All were ex-Californians. (Courtesy of the City of Vancouver Archives, B.C.; Mil–P. 79, Neg. 68)

(top) James Douglas, of African descent, on the day the new colony of British Columbia was established, being sworn in as its first governor, November 19, 1858. (Courtesy of the City of Vancouver Archives, B.C.; Out. P. 815, Neg. 373)

(left) Articles from *The Gazetteer* and *Guide*, published in Pittsburgh, Pennsylvania, which were widely circulated in Canada. A new exodus had begun. These reports were often greeted with enthusiasm when they concerned people moving into areas of low population. They were also viewed with alarm by some who thought that there were too many black people moving to Canada. (Courtesy of the City of Vancouver Archives, B.C.; general collection)

"creole" mother and John Douglas, a merchant, he was educated in Scotland. Back on the western coast of Canada, he married a young woman of Irish/Indian heritage and became a political leader.

Noted for his ability to communicate effectively with native Indians as well as the newcomers, he was popular and effective, although his autocratic style rankled many. Still, he is generally credited with using an imposing physical presence and powerful speaking skills to keep the United States from claiming more Canadian territory than it already had. So effective and persuasive was he that after the California trial of Archy Lee (which reinforced that state's support of slavery) Douglas advertised in California encouraging African Americans to move north to British Columbia. Those

The Gazetteer and Guide
A MONTHLY MAGAZINE.

JAMES A. ROSS, 25/4/03 EDITOR AND MANAGER.
J. H. LYNCH, ADVERTISING MANAGER.
OFFICE OF PUBLICATION, 183 CLINTON STREET,
BUFFALO, N. Y.
BRANCHES: Pittsburg, Philadelphia Montreal,
New York City, Cleveland, Chicago. St. Louis,
St. Paul, Toronto, Omaha and Portland, Ore.

An Opportunity for the Negro in Western Canada.

No better opportunity affords itself to the agricultural Negro than in Western Canada. And more especially those who live in the Southland and have a little capital. The one salvation of the Negro is to migrate to a section where he can be a component part in building up an undeveloped country under favorable conditions, there is no question to the fact, that it was largely the Negro labor that built up the Southland.' In this section of the country the farm hands are in demand land is cheap, and productive, the present indications are that it is unsafe for the Negro to continue to purchase property in the Southland. It is in our opinion a desperate chance to continue there deposits in the banks of that section. With a good strong arm a man can go to this section of Canada and in two years he can make enough money to send for his family, besides they can engage in agricultural pursuits taking up free grant lands, buying railway bonds or purchasing the improved farms to be found in advantageous positions in every province; or in mining they can secure employment in the manufacturing industries; or, if possessed of a settled income, living will be found to be much cheaper in Canada with the benefits of a fine, healthy climate, magnificent scenery, abundant opportunities for investments, and facilities for education and placing children in life not to be excelled any where; that is, those who have agricultural experience can succeed without doubt.

MORE NEGROES COMING TO SETTLE IN ALBERTA

Twenty More Farmers Are On the Way to Join the Colony

Edmonton 12/4/11

Guthrie. Okla., April 11.—The exodus of negroes from this state to Alberta which started several months ago, is continuing, despite the fact that it is not being encouraged by the Canadian government. Twenty negro farmers from near Fallis. Lincoln county, left here last night to join the colony in Alberta. They expect to take claims and immediately build homes and start their crops. after which their families. numbering in all about two hundred persons, will join them. It is said here that a colonization company is financing the negroes during the first months.

GENERAL EXODUS OF NEGROES INTO CANADA

Movement Follows Colonizing Campaign by Canadian Representatives During Winter Months.

OKLAHOMA CITY, March 26.—The final action of the Canadian government in admitting to that country negro families from Oklahoma is having the effect of further colonization movement among the negroes, especially in Okfuskee, Muskogee and Creek counties, where there is a heavy negro popoulation and several exclusive negro towns.

The first emigration to Canada during the past week was of ninety families, perhaps 500 negroes in all, from Okfuskee county. They sold all their property in this state, intending to homestead quarter section claims in Canada. Many other negroes are making preparations to start and indications are there will be a general exodus. It develops that the Canadian colonization work among the negroes has been in progress for several months, the intention being to move 1,000 families, or about 7,000 negroes, this spring, of which the Clearview emigrants formed the advance guard. It is understood a treaty provision admits them to Canada if they have $5 each in cash.

The emigrants as a rule are educated negroes, many of whom were taught in the government schools for Indians in old Indian Territory. They are leaving Oklahoma because of adverse legislation, "Jim Crow" coach and depot laws, the "grandfather clause" act that prohibits them from voting, separate school laws and others.

The Gazetteer and Guide, March 26, 1903
Page 6

Western Alberta, Canada, circa 1890, indicating major black settlements.

who did move were so happy with their decision that over a period of years several hundred more migrated.

The African Canadian pioneers established a pattern for the thousands of like-minded individuals to copy who moved to Canada over the following two hundred years.

"Hundreds of thousands of pioneers from the Middle West have crossed the national boundary into Canadian wheat fields eager to find farms for their children." So wrote Frederick Jackson Turner in his book *The Frontier in American History* ([1929] 1986, 227).

In an earlier chapter on the Plains states, Bill Blakey's family saga was recounted. Other members of the Blakey family were drawn to the western

United States by promises of rich farmland and a freedom that they had never experienced. However, when they reached South Dakota, either they sensed the presence of tensions similar to those of an earlier time or they heard of the land of "amber waves of grain" farther north in Alberta. For reasons not fully known today, they moved on, answering the distant call that had attracted many before them. They went to Athabasca Landing, Junkins (Wildwood), Alberta, and eventually changed the common name of the area to Amber Valley.

Martha Jane "Mattie" Mayes also found the lure of Canada's prairies too irresistible to ignore. She was born a slave on the Jesse Partridge plantation near Atlanta, Georgia, around 1847, and was a young girl when her master went into hiding and left the property under the direction of Mattie's grand-father. The subsequent Civil War battles left the plantation in ruins; Par-

Mattie Mayes, circa 1915, an early pioneer in Alberta. (Courtesy of the Saskatchewan Provincial Archives, Regina)

tridge returned only long enough to declare the farm a failure. Emancipation and the war had destroyed him, and he left the newly freed slaves to fend for themselves. Mattie's family moved to Tennessee, where she met and married Joseph Mayes.

Three years later the young couple moved to Oklahoma, starting a family at the time of the land rushes in that part of the country. They grew dissatisfied with the area, and began planning a northward migration after seeing a promotional advertisement for a move to Canada. Joseph had wanted such a move, and Mattie saw the northward migration as prophetic, because, in her words, "God freed us."

The "us" heading north were Joseph, Mattie, and ten children. Mattie was fifty-two years old. Taking a circuitous route through Tulsa, Oklahoma, and on to St. Paul, Minnesota, and then to Winnipeg, Regina, and Saskatoon, they made their way to Battleford, where they filed a claim in Maidstone, in the Eldon district.

Next, by oxcart, the family journeyed to their homestead and began farming, which they continued to do through the 1920s and 1930s. Three more children were born to this couple who had become the center of the Eldon settlement.

Joseph died in the 1920s; and Mattie, at the age of 104, died in March 1953. The family's migratory path crossed the entire span of slavery and led to freedom in a new land.

The Underground Railroad had several final destination points, but one of the most important—and long-lasting—settlements was at North Buxton, Ontario. Located on a fertile plain in Raleigh Township, the village was established in 1849 under the leadership of Reverend William King. In short order, the town had grown to approximately 1,500 individuals, virtually all of them runaway slaves from the States.

Unlike many other settlements of this type, Elgin had a strong economy, based on booming agricultural production plus the added stability of permanent employment with the trans-Canadian Railway. The latter allowed workers to purchase land and turn homesteads into permanent family residences.

The American Civil War was a clarion call to many of the settlers who returned to the States solely to fight the South. Their stories are legendary.

Abraham Doras Shadd was the progenitor of one of the most influential families to have roots in the Buxton community. Born a slave in 1801 to parents Jeremiah and Amelia (Cisco) Shadd, Abraham moved with his brother Absalom from Delaware to Pennsylvania in 1833. Later they would relocate to Buxton, Raleigh Township, Ontario, around 1850.

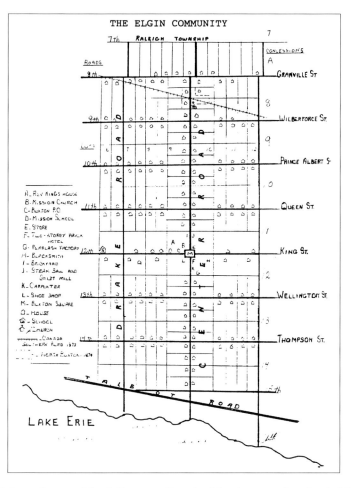

The Elgin settlement, North Buxton, Ontario. No photographs of early North Buxton (Elgin community) exist. But this town map hints at its size and complexity. (Courtesy of the Raleigh Township Memorial Museum, North Buxton, Ontario)

A close friend of Reverend Josiah Henson (ostensibly the source of stories used in Harriet Beecher Stowe's Uncle Tom's Cabin), Shadd soon became a strong political voice in the village, serving on the Raleigh Township Council. He met on occasion with the American abolitionist John Brown, who often visited and lectured in the area. In his spare time he established Masonic Lodges throughout Lower Canada.

Shadd had married Harriet Parnell before moving to Buxton; together

(left) Abraham D. Shadd, circa 1860. Political, religious, and social leader of the Buxton Community in Ontario. (Courtesy of the Raleigh Township Memorial Museum, North Buxton, Ontario)

(right) Abraham W. Shadd, circa 1885, in his Civil War uniform. Like many African Canadians, he served proudly as a volunteer for the Union army. (Courtesy of the Raleigh Township Memorial Museum, North Buxton, Ontario)

they eventually raised thirteen children, many of whom became the most influential citizens of their time in that part of Canada.

One of Abraham's oldest children, Abraham W., was a teenager when he returned again to the States (his place of birth in 1844). He stayed behind when his father and uncle returned to Canada. He became a lawyer, served with the Northern military during the Civil War, stationed in Mississippi as a member of the Twenty-Fourth Kent Militia from Canada, who were volunteers for the Union. Shadd rose to the rank of Captain of the One-Hundred-Fourth Colored Troops, and served as an aide and clerk to Major Martin R. Delaney.

He married Selina in Louisiana, circa 1870, and the couple had two children, Abraham and Selina M. He returned with his family to Elgin, where he was baptized in 1874.

Mary Shadd Cary, author, teacher, abolitionist, journalist. (Courtesy of the Raleigh Township Memorial Museum, North Buxton, Ontario)

The eldest of the senior Abraham's children was Mary Ann Camberton Shadd, born when the family was living free in Wilmington, Delaware. The family was deeply involved in the Underground Railroad, and it was an experience that would shape her life

When Mary was ten, she went with her family to West Chester, Pennsylvania, near Philadelphia. It was at that time that the most important educational experience of her life took place: schooling in a Quaker institution. Abraham had joined the Religious Society of Friends when he became active in the National Convention for the Improvement of Free People of Color in the United States and the American Anti-Slavery Society. Mary witnessed the revolutionary zeal of her father and that of the society's as she attended classes in the rigorous environment of a Friends school.

Mary grew up in an environment of radical abolitionist sentiment, led and fueled by her father and his friends, all of whom subscribed to Nat Turner's arguments and William Lloyd Garrison's Liberator—a newspaper so strong in its views that in many cities black people (free, in name only) were forbidden by law to carry it from their post offices.

> What of the four millions of colored people in the entire South? . . . The American Government is but a mockery and deserves to be overthrown, if they are to be left without protection, as sheep in the midst of wolves . . . . Let the edict go forth, trumpet-tongued, that there shall be a speedy end put to this bloody misrule.
>
> (William Lloyd Garrison, *The Liberator*, December 29, 1865)

When she was fourteen, the family and the community was shaken by the murder of Elijah P. Lovejoy, editor and pioneering antislavery writer in Alton, Illinois. Lovejoy was a personal friend of the family and a founding member of the Anti-Slavery Society. His death had a profound impact on the family. Clearly, Lovejoy's death was a catalytic event in her life and turned her toward careers in teaching and writing.

When she was thirty-three years old, the family—fed up with the slow pace of racial reform in the States—headed for western Canada, and Mary Shadd began her historic career. This remarkable woman would become a schoolteacher and principal in several schools, politician, campaigner for women's rights, a recruiting officer in America's Civil War, the first African American woman to study law at Howard University, author, practicing lawyer, mother, and proselytizer for the cause of freedom and editor of *The Provincial Freeman* (Windsor, Toronto, and Chatham, Canada)—the first black woman in North America to have such a career.

Jamaican and West Indian Immigration

Nearly concurrent with the time that American blacks were fighting for and being granted their emancipation, Jamaican and West Indian immigrants were facing their own crises in Canada. Many Canadians feared the political power that black immigrants from America might wield in their Parliament. So, to constrain that potential influence, the governing body attempted to pass a law declaring that black immigrants could acquire full rights of citizenship only after a five-year waiting period. This provision would depress the influence of American blacks, but would not impact Jamaicans, since they were British by birth.

Julius Isaac, immigrant from Grenada, who was appointed chief justice of the Federal Court of Canada, December 1991. Isaac was typical, in many ways, of the caliber of Jamaican immigrants into Canada. (Courtesy of the Caribbean Association of Manitoba, Canada)

The enmity left over from this attempt to divide and conquer black citizens would have a lasting impact on intraracial relations for many years—as well as serve to divide their political influences over an emotional issue.

Suffice it to say, Jamaicans began migrating to Canada in the nineteenth century, their numbers rose dramatically in the early twentieth century and continue to this day.

CHAPTER FOURTEEN

THE UTENDALE/SHAW/BOYD TREK NORTH

Most black families are poorly recorded in the annals of Canada, just as they are difficult to trace in the States.[1] Although many were literate, many moved into areas that were remote, primitive, and lacking systematized record keeping.

The urge to migrate to lands offering more opportunity than the place of origin does is as old as time. A chance to improve one's lot, escape privations, or to find adventure and romance will, in all likelihood, continue to be the moving force. But specific evidence of such changes is sometimes difficult to find.

Occasionally, however, both records and photographs are preserved. Such is the case with the Shaw/Utendale/Boyd families of western Canada. They provide a rare case study of outward migration from the United States and

---

1. I am especially indebted to the following individuals for the material in this chapter: Dr. Kent Utendale of Vancouver, British Columbia; Morris and Yvonne Boyd of Edmonton, Alberta; and Lemuel Boyd and Carol Lafayette-Boyd of Regina, Saskatchewan. Without the generous help of these descendants, this chapter could never have been written.

(left) "Wildwood" School, Junkins, Alberta, c. 1923. Home and school to many black settlers in the early part of the twentieth century. (Courtesy of Morris and Yvonne Boyd, Edmonton, Alberta.)

Lucretia Armstrong in Anadarko, Oklahoma, circa 1880, on the Cherokee reservation. A Cherokee "princess," Lucretia would help found a family whose descendants live today all across western Canada. (Courtesy of Dr. Kent Utendale, Vancouver, B.C.)

Europe, as well as pioneering spirits that are remarkable for their strength and endurance.

As with most early African Canadian families, the story begins several generations ago with Lucretia, a Cherokee "princess" who married Timothy Armstrong in Oklahoma, probably around Anadarko. She died young and never went to Canada. However, she was the progenetrix of a family that would help populate three western Canadian provinces.

Standing over six feet tall, Timothy Armstrong[2] was a slave to the Cherokees (a subjugation more common to Plains Indians than those of Oklahoma, but certainly a possibility). Praised by the Indians for his skill in

2. Slaves and ex-slaves often took the names of their masters, so it is not unusual that Timothy would have adopted the name of Strong Arm to honor the Cherokees who had taken him in.

Timothy Armstrong in Anadarko, Oklahoma, circa 1880. His surname is an inversion of his Cherokee name, Strong Arm. It would become his family's surname. (Courtesy of Dr. Kent Utendale, Vancouver, B.C.)

hunting and battle, he was freed by them and accepted as a member of the group. A rugged, dark-skinned man,[3] Timothy married Lucretia and they began a family.

Lucretia and Timothy had two daughters, Lily and Millie, and one son, James. Timothy favored his son over the girls, who were apparently left to their own devices. Lily was raised by her older sister Millie on the Cherokee reservation near Anadarko, Oklahoma. It was at this time that members of the family went their separate ways.

According to present-day members of the family, Lily was just as individualistic and dynamic as her picture suggests. She was born in Oletha,

3. Timothy's image does not seem that of a dark-skinned man. However, daguerreotypes were commonly tinted, bleached, or otherwise altered by the studio to suit the demands of customers.

Lily Armstrong Shaw's wedding picture, circa 1898. Standing barely four feet tall, Lily married the equally short—and equally pugnacious—Rollie Shaw prior to moving from Kansas to Canada around the turn of the century. (Courtesy of Dr. Kent Utendale, Vancouver, B.C.)

Kansas, in 1882. Her older sister Millie died relatively young, as did their mother, Lucretia. Lily often described living in a sod house in Kansas, picking cotton, and going to school in a one-room schoolhouse.

In her twenties, the strong-willed Lily fell in love with a Mississippi riverboat gambler, but she was restrained by her parents. They directed her attentions toward someone they perceived as a more suitable mate, Walter Rolly Shaw, who owned (with his father) a nice, solid furniture business—and, her parents remarked, had lighter skin.

To her dying day, she lamented the fact that she had married Walter and

Walter Rolly Shaw's wedding picture. Just as Lily's wedding picture revealed striking characteristics, this one displays Rollie's devil-may-care attitude and unique personality. (Courtesy of Dr. Kent Utendale, Vancouver, B.C.)

moved to Alberta, Canada, leaving her friends behind and severing her relations with those she loved on the reservation.

The marriage took place around the turn of the century and the young couple moved to Junkins (today's Wildwood), Alberta, in 1908, when Lily was twenty-six years old. When she was twenty-eight, she bore the first of their four children, Alberta, Thomas, Ruth Mae, and James. The first three children were born in Junkins, which was a "black town." Although she never learned to read or write, her grandchildren remember her as lively and creative, her days filled with whimsy and delight.

Rufus Shaw, in front of his store in Anadarko, Oklahoma, circa 1895. Anadarko, like many small towns in that state, beckoned to a large number of African Americans during those times. The sign above the door reads, "Rufus Shaw Furniture Bought and Sold." (Courtesy of Dr. Kent Utendale, Vancouver, B.C.)

Walter Rolly Shaw traveled the same roads taken by other young black men of his time. Born in 1880 in Nashville, Tennessee, he was named after Sir Walter Raleigh, but his parents didn't know how the middle name was spelled. His father was an Irishman from County Cork, Ireland; his mother was a black woman from Tennessee.

Walter's father, Rufus, was a successful businessman, which subsequently earned him the unwanted attention of the local Klu Klux Klan. On trumped-up charges that Rufus had raped a white women, the Klan threatened to lynch him. The family hid in a root cellar while Klansmen ranted and raved around them. Whether their plan was to kill Rufus or not is not known, but the effect was to motivate Walter to move away from that environment as soon as he could.

Like many others, Walter and his brothers searched from California to the Midwest for more promising possibilities in life than what was on their immediate horizon. Unlike many others, however, this man at five feet, three inches showed a determination to live and prosper. It was not an auspicious time for the timid. Noted for his inability to hold liquor, Walter

Walter Rolley Shaw's sisters, Janie and Maggie Shaw, in Anadarko, Oklahoma, circa 1890. Maggie (seated) was approximately twenty-five years old and Janie was sixteen. (Courtesy of Dr. Kent Utendale, Vancouver, B.C.)

Amber Valley, British Columbia. Named after the fabled "amber waves of grain" promised in the States, this land lies fifteen miles east of Athabasca in Alberta. This verdant, rolling area lured black homesteaders to western Canada from 1890 to the 1920s. (Photo by J. W. Ravage, summer 1996)

The Athabasca River flows through the town of Athabasca, Alberta. Also a railhead and a landing on the river, the site was a jumping-off place for immigrant Ukrainians, Russians, and African-American pioneers from the States. (Photo by J. W. Ravage, summer 1996)

Junkins (now, Wildwood), Alberta. In northern Alberta, west of Edmonton, this area was settled circa 1900, prior to Amber Valley. Shown is the family of Tony Paine, one of its earliest pioneers. (Courtesy of Dr. Kent Utendale, Vancouver, B.C.)

shot up more than one bar in his time. (A note of interest: one cousin worked for Jessie James's mother. It was a time in which tough characters were responsible for violent actions.) Before Walter married Lily, he had fallen under a train, languished in a coma, lost both index fingers, and had a hole in his cranium closed with a metal plate. To top it off, he was also run over by a motorcycle and given last rites.

Then he met Lily.

Oklahoma was granted statehood and immediately introduced legislation to disenfranchise African Americans. The handwriting was on the wall, and shortly after Walter and Lily married, he decided to look elsewhere for a place to live. The poor economic and social environment of the state—let alone the festering memories of what the Klan could do—drove him to check out the greener fields in Manitoba, specifically, and Canada, in general. One trip north convinced them that, no matter how attractive the open lands of Manitoba were, the cold was too great for them.

They headed next for central Alberta and the settlement of Junkins. Joining a large group of black men and women, they moved in 1908 to Junkins—

100 miles west of Edmonton—whose fertile fields would prove to be the final attraction.

While pioneering in what had come to be called Wildwood, Lily and Walter branched out from their farming operation to run a grocery store to help support their four children. All became pioneering Canadians on their own; their children and grandchildren live today in Alberta, British Columbia, and Saskatchewan.

At different times, Lily would remark to family members that she always regretted leaving the States; but she would also tell of the hated snakes and insects and the night-riding Klansmen and describe the terrible living conditions on and around the Indian reservation. She was a fascinating storyteller, possessing a strong personality to her last days—and nights, in which she slept with a hammer next to her bed to ward off the evil horsemen who still might come charging out of her memories.

Walter died of a stroke in 1962 when he was eighty-two. Before that he had spent much of his time racing around town on his ancient double-barred bicycle, often not avoiding accidents. Lily lived four years longer than Walter. She died saying, "I want to go to my grave so I can be with Walter again."

The move northward to join other black families around Edmonton and the towns of Junkins (then Wildwood) and Athabasca Landing (generally considered the Amber Valley area) brought together a large number of men, women and children, mostly from the States. But there were others who came from farther away.

Alfred and Susannah Utendale met in London near the turn of the century. He was the son of a Norwegian sea captain who had married a half-white, half—East Indian woman. Susannah was most likely Jewish. They had two children, Pretoria and Alfred, Jr., shortly before they immigrated to Canada. They homesteaded in Maidstone, Saskatchewan. Within a decade they had moved to Edmonton.

In those days, the couple was considered to be "West Indian" rather than "coloured," a less acceptable appellation, perhaps because of her northern English accent and his admixture of three foreign languages. Whatever the reason or cause, their integration into the new land was complete.

Alfred, Jr., married a woman whose parental heritage was Norwegian, English, and Guinean. Not unlike in the Hawaiian Islands, the citizens of Saskatchewan and Alberta apparently paid little attention to exotic appearances and backgrounds, in contrast to their neighbors to the south, in the States.

From left to right: Iva Perrot, Barkley Boyd, Sadie Miller, prior to their moving
to Alberta around 1900 with their mother, Letha Boyd. Their father stayed in
the States. Barkley Boyd would marry Alberta Shaw, thereby joining two
pioneering families. (Courtesy of Morris and Yvonne Boyd, Edmonton, Alberta)

One of Alfred, Jr.,'s children, Ruhamah, was the first African Canadian
teacher in Alberta, the first woman to teach in southern British Columbia,
and the first school principal in British Columbia.

The Kelly family of Oklahoma, later of Alberta, Canada, were the chil-
dren of Letha Boyd. More typical than not of immigrant families of the
times, the Kellys reflect highly mixed racial and ethnic backgrounds: Joe
Perrot married Iva Boyd, whose sister Ella had previously married George
Kelly. Barkely Boyd's sister, "Aunt Atha," married a Chinese man, John
Lee. Their son Wilbert married a Polish woman as his first bride and an

Alfred and Susannah Utendale, London, England, circa 1898. Alfred, whose parents were Norwegians, married a London woman, prior to moving to Canada. (Courtesy of Dr. Kent Utendale, Vancouver, B.C.)

The Kelly family, settlers in Alberta, shown in Oklahoma, circa 1905, before migrating north. Of mixed racial heritage, they joined other pioneers in the area to establish early towns. (Courtesy of Morris and Yvonne Boyd, Edmonton, Alberta)

English woman in a second marriage. This family is but one colorful example of married life on the Canadian Plains at the turn of the century.

The towns, previously mentioned, that harbored these men, women, and children waxed and waned over a period of nearly one hundred years. Some families moved on to larger cities and better employment oppotunities. Their sons, daughters, and grandchildren almost never felt the urge to move back to the States, to where their ancestors once lived. These new citizens found Canada to be all that the earlier pioneers had dreamed of: a land of kept promises, with great stretches of rich earth—a fine place to live, raise children, and grow old together.

AFTERWORD

Rising out of servitude and bondage, black men and women did not cease their accomplishments with the turn of the twentieth century. Clearly, their achievements continue to this day and have become part of American history. As a result, the term "black history" is now a misnomer to many, fused forever into the true chronicles of our nation's past.

Couched in a four-hundred-year-old legacy of enslavement based on skin color, persons of African descent still face challenges not placed before the bulk of North Americans. Prejudice continues to permeate the social and political systems of the United States and Canada, though few would argue that it is as intense as what has gone before. However, only the most pollyanna-ish among us would argue that mistreatment, distortion, and inequities have disappeared.

(left) "The Freed Slave," a statue created for the Columbian Exposition in 1892, St. Louis, Missouri. Seen here in *The Illustrated History of the Great Exposition, 1892*, is a nineteenth-century allegorical image of a "new black man," set free from bondage. (From author's collection)

"Mushing the Trail," in Alaska, circa 1880. (Photo by W. H. Jackson; courtesy of the United States Geological Survey Photographic Archives, Denver, Colorado)

Change is natural, and a changing view of the past is part of the present. As we collect more information about what has been witheld, misinterpreted, overlooked, or otherwise hidden from our view, we are brought to a more complete understanding of the issues. In that respect, this book began with references to the western historian Frederick Jackson Turner who argued that what we call "the West" is a unique product of the various social and ethnic groups who pioneered west of the Mississippi River. What resulted, the "development" of an American society, was the product of not only white immigrants from Europe but also a singular combination of Native Americans, Asians, Spanish and Mexican immigrants, African sons and daughters, and subgroups so numerous as to beggar enumeration. We are truly a nation of transplanted foreigners; it is the scope of this fact that makes us a modern nation unlike others.

These pioneering men and women overcame barriers that most of us can only imagine; ironically, they are ones that contributed to a unique character called "American." In the midst of these events, the French historian

William Faux visited western areas in the early 1800s and remarked about the new nation's weaknesses and strengths:

> Finally; were, however, America, of which I now perhaps take my leave for ever, everything that the purest patriotism could make it, yet the climate is an evil, a perpetual evil, a mighty drawback, an almost insurmountable obstacle to the health, wealth, and well-being of all, except the native red and black man, the genuine aboriginal, and the unstained African, for whom alone this land of promise, this vast section of the earth, this new and better world, seems by nature to have been intended.
>
> (Faux 1826, 137)

Faux knew that exploring and moving to new lands, and bringing new energies to them, is what humankind has done for all of its existence. It is the resultant infusion of energy, innovation, determination, and character that carried not only black men and women westward but also gave this nation its vitality.

LIST OF COLLECTIONS

A work such as this could only be accomplished with the aid of dedicated, helpful, and cheerful curators and archivists. Following is a list of collections used in this text. Most are museums and libraries; some are operated by individuals. It is with great gratitude and appreciation that they are acknowledged.

Alaska State Archives, Juneau
American Heritage Center, University of Wyoming, Laramie
Amon Carter Museum, Fort Worth, Texas
Anchorage Museum of History and Art, Akaska
Anchorage Public Library, Alaska
Arizona Historical Society, Phoenix
William Bailey III, Edgemont, South Dakota
Barry Goldwater Collection, Arizona Historical Foundation, Tempe
Ben E. Pingenot Collection, Brackettville, Texas
Bishop Museum, Honolulu, Hawaii
The Black American West Museum and Heritage Center, Denver, Colorado
Ted Blakey, Yankton, South Dakota
Lemuel and Carolyn Boyd, Regina, Saskatchewan
Morris and Yvonne Boyd, Edmonton, Alberta
California State Library, Sacramento
Caribbean Association of Manitoba, Canada

Church of Jesus Christ of Latter-day Saints Historical Department, Salt Lake City, Utah
City of Oakland, California
City of Sacramento Archives, California
City of Vancouver Archives, British Columbia
Coe Library, Reference Section, University of Wyoming, Laramie
Collins Street Bakery, Corsicana, Texas
Colorado State Historical Society, Denver
Denver Public Library, Western History Collection, Denver
Dick Perue Historical Photos, Saratoga, Wyoming
Fort Huachuca, Arizona
Fort Robinson State Park, Crawford, Nebraska
Fort Sill Museum, Oklahoma
Fort Verde State Park, Arizona
The Gilcrease Museum, Tulsa, Oklahoma
W. Gordon Gillespie, Laramie, Wyoming
Glenbow Museum, Calgary, Alberta
Grant City Museum, Canyon City, Oregon
Great Plains Black Museum, Omaha, Nebraska
Ralph Hayes, Seattle, Washington
Haynes Foundation Collection, Montana Historical Society, Helena
Hawaii State Archives, Honolulu, Hawaii
Idaho State Historical Society, Boise
Institute of Texan Cultures, San Antonio
J. Guthrie Nicholson, Jr., Collection, American Heritage Center, University of Wyoming, Laramie
John Slaughter State Park, Arizona
Kansas State Historical Society, Topeka
Beatrice Kercherval, Edgemont, South Dakota
LaFrantz Collection, American Heritage Center, University of Wyoming, Laramie
Lahaina Whaling Museum and Rick Ralston, Hawaii
Latah County Historical Society, Moscow, Idaho
Lewis County Historical Museum, Chehalis, Washington
Library of Congress, Washington, D.C.
Little Big Horn National Monument, Crow Agency, Montana
Miriam Matthews Collection, California African-American Museum, Los Angeles
Mission House Museum Library, Honolulu, Hawaii
Montana State Historical Society, Helena
Moorland-Spinyarn Research Collection, Howard University, Washington, D.C.

Museum of New Mexico, Santa Fe
Mystic Seaport Museum, Connecticut
National Archives, Washington, D.C.
National Park Service, Anchorage, Alaska
Nebraska State Historical Society, Lincoln
Nevada State Historical Society, Reno
North Dakota State Historical Society, Bismarck
Northern California Center for Afro American Historical Museum, Oakland
Oregon Historical Society, Portland
Peter Palmquist, Arvata, California
Providence Public Library Archives, Rhode Island
Raleigh Township Memorial Museum, North Buxton, Ontario, Canada
Rasmussen Collection, University of Alaska Archives, Fairbanks
R. W. Graves Collection, Chadron State University Library, Nebraska
San Francisco Public Library, San Francisco
Saskatchewan Provincial Archives, Regina
Savery Museum, Wyoming
Sharlott Hall Museum, Prescott, Arizona
John Slaughter Ranch and Harvey Finks, Arizona
Smithsonian Institute, Washington, D.C.
South Dakota State Historical Society, Pierre
Spokane Northwest Black Pioneers, Washington
Spokane Public Library, Spokane, Washington
Sweetwater County Library, Green River, Wyoming
Teton County Historical Society, Jackson, Wyoming
Thermopolis Museum, Wyoming
Tulia Museum, Texas
Tuskegee University Archives, Alabama
United States Geological Survey Photographic Archives, Denver, Colorado
University of Nevada, Reno
University of North Dakota, Grand Forks
University of Wyoming Library, Reference Section, Laramie
Ursuline Centre, Great Falls, Montana
Dr. Kent Utendale, Vancouver, British Columbia
William Hallam Webber, Rockville, Maryland
Western Kentucky State University Archives, Bowling Green
The White House Collection, Washington, D.C
Woolarock State Parks, Oklahoma
Wyoming State Museum and Archive, Cheyenne
Yellowstone National Park Archives, Mammoth, Wyoming
X.I.T. Museum, Dalhart, Texas

.

BIBLIOGRAPHY

Addington, Wendell G. 1950. "Slave Insurrections in Texas." *The Journal of Negro History* 35:408–34.

Adler, Mortimer, ed. 1969. *The Negro in American History.* New York, N.Y.: Encyclopedia Britannica Educational Corporation.

The Afro-American Texans. 1987. San Antonio: Institute for Texan Cultures.

Aldrich, Herbert L. 1889. *Arctic Alaska and Siberia, or Eight Months with the Arctic Whalemen.* Chicago, Ill., and New York. N.Y.: Rand, McNally.

Ambrose, Stephen E. 1996. *Undaunted Courage.* New York, N.Y.: Simon and Schuster.

Amherstberg Regular Missionary Baptist Association. 1940. "A History of the Amherstberg Regular Missionary Baptist Association, Its Auxiliaries and Churches." Compiled from minutes taken by members. Amherstberg, Ontario, Canada.

Amos, Preston E. 1974. *Above and Beyond in the West, Black Medal of Honor Winners.* Falls Church, Va.: Pioneer America Society Press.

Andrew, John A., III. n.d. Betsy Stockton: Stranger in a Strange Land. *Journal of Presbyterian History,* unnumbered:157–65.

Andrews, Clarence L. 1937. *The Pioneers and the Nuggets of Verse They Penned from the Graves of the Past.* Seattle, Wash.: Luke Tinker, Commercial Printer.

Aptheker, Herbert. 1948. *To Be Free: Studies in American Negro History.* New York, N.Y.: International Publishers.

_____. 1938. *The Negro in the Civil War.* New York, N.Y.: International Publishers.

Athearn, Robert G. 1978. *In Search of Canaan: Black Migration to Kansas, 1879–1880.* Lawrence, Kans.: The Regents Press of Kansas.

Bailey, Linda C. 1997. *Fort Missoula's Military Cyclists: The Story of the 25th. U.S. Infantry Bicycle Corps.* (Monograph.) Missoula, Mont.: The Friends of the Historical Museum at Fort Missoula.

Baltich, Frances. 1982. *Search for Safety: The Founding of Stockton's Black Commu-nity.* Stockton, Calif.: F. Baltich.

Barbeau, Arthur E., and Florett Henri. 1974. *The Unknown Soldiers.* Philadelphia, Pa.: Temple University Press.

Barbosa, Steven. 1994. *Door of No Return: The Legend of Goree Island.* Dutton, N.Y.: Cobblehill Books.

Bardolph, Richard. 1959. *The Negro Vanguard.* New York, N.Y.: Rinehart.

Barnum, Francis. 1893. *Life on the Alaska Mission.* Baltimore, Md.: Woodstock College Press.

Barrow, Robert, and Leigh Hambly. 1988. *Billy: The Life and Photographs of William S. A. Beal.* Winnipeg, Manitoba, Canada: Vig. Corps Press.

Bearden, Jim, and Linda Jean Butler. 1977. *The Life and Times of Mary Shadd Cary.* Toronto, Ontario, Canada: N.C. Press, Ltd.

Beasley, Delilah L. 1919. *The Negro Trailblazers of California.* Los Angeles, Calif.: Times Mirror Printing and Binding House.

Beckwourth, James P. 1856. *The Life and Adventures of James T. Beckwourth: Mountaineer, Scout, and Pioneer.* Edited by T. D. Bonner. New York, N.Y.: Harper and Brothers.

Beller, Jack. 1929. "Negro Slaves in Utah." *Utah Historical Quarterly* 2:122–26.

Bergmann, Leola Nelson. 1969. *The Negro in Iowa.* Iowa City, Iowa: The State Historical Society of Iowa.

Bernson, Sara L., and Robert J. Eggers. 1977. "Black People in South Dakota History." *South Dakota History* 7 (Summer):241–70.

Bertley, Leo W. 1977. *Canada and Its People of African Descent.* Pierrefonds, Que-bec, Canada: Bilongo Publishers.

Betts, Robert B. 1985. *In Search of York.* Boulder, Colo.: Colorado Associated University Press.

Beyer, Audrey White. 1968. *Dark Venture* (a novel). New York, N.Y.: Alfred A. Knopf.

"Black Hills Rancher." 1954. *Ebony* 9 (October):16–20.

Blasingame, Ike. 1958. *Dakota Cowboy: My Life in the Old Days.* New York,

N.Y.: G.P. Putnam's Sons.

"Bloodline That Will Never Lose It's [sic] Power." 1985. Unpublished, unattributed monograph of the Blakey/Blakely/White family, July. Yankton, S.D.

Bockstoce, John R. 1986. *Whales, Ice, and Men*. Seattle, Wash: University of Washington Press.

Bolster, William Jeffrey. 1990. "To Feel Like a Man." *Journal of American History* 76 (March):1173–99.

Brawley, Benjamin. 1950. *A Short History of the American Negro*. 4th ed., rev. New York, N.Y.: Macmillan.

Broussard, Albert S. 1990. Carlotta Stewart Lai, a Black Teacher in the Territory of Hawai'i. *The Hawai'ian Journal of History* 24:129–53.

Buecker, Thomas. 1984. "Confrontation at Sturgis." *South Dakota History* 14 (Fall):238–61.

_____. 1991. "The 10th Cavalry at Ft. Robinson: Black Troops in the West, 1902–1907." *Military Images* 12 (May-June):6.

Bundy, Hallock C. 1910. *The Valdez-Fairbanks Trail*. Seattle, Wash.: Alaska Publishing.

Burkett, Randall K. 1991. *Black Biography, 1790–1950*. Alexandria, Va.: Chadwick-Healy.

Burton, Arthur. 1991. *Black, Red, and Deadly: Black and Indian Gunfighters of the Indian Territories*. Eakin, Tx.: Eakin Press.

_____. 1992. "Bass Reeves: A Legendary Lawman of the Western Frontier." *Persimmon Hill* 20 (2):45–48.

Busch, Briton Cooper. 1994. *Whaling Will Never Do for Me*. Lexington, Ky.: University Press of Kentucky.

Bustard, Bruce I. 1993. *Western Ways: Images of the American West*. Washington, D.C.: National Archives and Records Administration.

Butler, William Francis. 1915. *The Wild North Land*. London, England: Burns and Oates.

Calabretta, Fred. 1993. "The Picture of Antoine DeSant" *The Log of Mystic Seaport* 44 (4):93–95.

Carlson, Paul H. 1989. *"Pecos Bill": A Military Biography of William H. Carlson*. College Station, Tx.: Texas A&M University Press.

Carroll, John M. 1971. *The Black Military Experience in the American West*. New York, N.Y.: Liveright Publishing.

Carter, Kate B. 1965. *The Story of the Negro Pioneer*. Salt Lake City, Ut.: Daughters of the Utah Pioneers.

Carter, Velma Thorne, and Wanda Leffler-Akill. 1981. *The Window of Our Memories*. St. Albert, Alberta, Canada: B.C.R. Society of Alberta.

Cashin, Herschel V. 1899. *Under Fire with the Tenth Cavalry*. London, England, and New York, N.Y.: Tennyson, Neely.

Chambers, Melvett G. 1986. *The Black History Trivia Book.* Denver, Colo.: Melvett Chambers.

Chase, Will H. 1951. *Pioneers of Alaska: Trailblazers of Bygone Days.* Kansas City, Mo.: Burton Publishing.

Chrisman, Harry E. 1961. *Lost Trails of the Cimarron.* Denver, Colo.: Alan Swallow.

Chu, Daniel, and Bill Shaw. 1994. *Going Home to Nicodemus.* Morristown, N.J.: Silver Burdett Press.

Clayton, Lawrence. 1992. Bill "Tige" Avery. In *Cowboys Who Rode Proudly,* edited by James Evetts Haley. Midland, Tx: Nita Stewart Haley Memorial Library.

Coates, Ken. 1992. *North to Alaska: 50 Years on the World's Most Remarkable Highway.* Anchorage, Alaska: University of Alaska Press.

Coe, George W. 1938. *Frontier Fighter: The Autobiography of George Coe, Who Fought and Rode with Billy the Kid, as Told to H. Hillary Harrison.* Albuquerque, N.M.: University of New Mexico Press.

Coffman, Edward M. 1986. *The Old Army: A Portrait of the American Army in Peacetime, 1784–1898.* New York, N.Y.: Oxford University Press.

Cohen, Stan. 1992. *The Trail of '42: A Pictorial History of the Alaska Highway.* Missoula, Mont.: Pictorial Histories Publishing.

Coleman, Ronald G. 1979. "The Buffalo Soldiers: Guardians of the Uintah Frontier 1886–1901." *Utah Historical Quarterly* 47(4):421–39.

_____. 1981. Blacks in Utah History: An Unknown Legacy. In *The Peoples of Utah.* Edited by Helen Z. Papanikolas. Salt Lake City, Utah: Utah State Historical Society.

Collings, Ellsworth, and Alma Miller England. 1938. *The 101 Ranch.* Norman, Okla.: University of Oklahoma Press.

Connelly, Christopher P. 1938. *The Devil Learns to Vote.* New York, N.Y.: Covici, Friede.

Cook, Fred J. 1957. "The Slave Ship Rebellion." *American Heritage* 8 (February):60–106.

Cooper, Gary. 1959. "Stage Coach Mary." *Ebony* 8 (October):97–100.

Cowley, Malcolm, ed. 1928. *The Adventures of an African Slaver.* Garden City, N.Y.: Garden City Publishing Co.

Crockett, Norman L. 1979. *The Black Towns.* Lawrence, Kans.: The Regents Press of Kansas.

Crouchett, Lawrence P., Lonnie G. Bunch III, and Martha Kendall Winnacker. 1989. *Visions toward Tomorrow: The History of the East Bay Afro-American Community, 1852–1977.* Oakland, Calif.: Northern California Center for Afro American History and Life.

Cruise of the Corwin, 1881. 1883. Washington, D.C.: U.S. Government Printing Office.

Curl, Caroline, ed. 1984. *Edgemont: The River, the Rails, the Ranch Lands.* Edgemont, S.D.: Edgemont Herald Tribune.

Daniels, Douglas Henry. 1991. *Pioneer Urbanites: A Social and Cultural History of Black San Francisco.* Berkeley, Calif.: University of California Press.

Dayton, Edson Carr. 1937. *Dakota Days.* Hartford, Conn.: Edson Carr Dayton.

DeGraaf, Lawrence B. 1975. "Recognition, Racism, and Reflections on the Writing of Western Black History." *Pacific Historical Review* 44 (February):22–51.

Dick, Everitt. 1937. *The Sod-House Frontier, 1854–1890.* New York, N.Y.: D. Appleton-Century.

Dixon, Thomas, Jr. 1903. *The Leopard's Spots: A Romance of the White Man's Burden, 1865–1900.* New York, N.Y.: Doubleday.

Donaldson, Lilian C., and Robert E. Williams. 1991. *The Donaldson Odyssey: Footsteps to Freedom.* Seattle, Wash.: Lilian C. Donaldson and Robert E. Williams.

Duncan, T. Bentley. 1972. *Atlantic Islands Madiera, the Azores and the Cape Verdes in Seventeenth-Century Commerce and Navigation.* Chicago, Ill.: The University of Chicago Press.

Durham, Philip. 1955. "The Negro Cowboy." *The Midwest Journal* 7:298–301.

_____, and Everett L. Jones. 1956. *The Negro Cowboys.* New York, N.Y.: Dodd, Mead.

Edwards, Malcolm. 1977. "The War of Complexional Distinction: Blacks in Gold Rush California and British Columbia." *California Historical Quarterly* 56 (Spring):34–45.

Ege, Robert. 1966. "Isaiah Dorman: Negro Casualty With Reno." *Montana Western History* 16 (January):35–40.

Emilio, Luis F. 1891. *History of the Fifty-Fourth Regiment of the Massachusetts Volunteer Infantry, 1863–1865.* Boston, Mass.: Boston Company.

Ernst, Robert. 1954. "Negro Concepts of Americanism." *Journal of Negro History* 39:206–19.

Evans, John Thomas (né James Williams). 1874. *Life and Adventures of James Williams: A Fugitive Slave.* San Francisco, Calif.: Women's Union Print.

Everette, Oliver Page. 1965. *God Has Been Northward Always.* Seattle, Wash.: Bradley Printing and Lithograph.

Everitt, Dick. 1937. *The Sod-House Frontier, 1854–1890.* New York, N.Y.: D. Appleton-Century Co.

Farr, James Barker. 1989. *Black Odyssey: The Seafaring Traditions of Afro-Ameri-*

cans. Ph.D. diss. Ann Arbor, Mich.: University Microfilms.

Faux, William. 1826. Memorable Days in America. In *Early Western Travels, 1748–1846,* vol. 12. Edited by Reuben Gold Thwaites. Cleveland, Ohio: Arthur H. Clark.

Fishwick, Marshall, ed. 1971. *Remus, Rastus, and Revolution.* Bowling Green, Ohio: Bowling Green University Popular Press.

_____. 1974. *The Black Soldier and Officer in the United States Army, 1891–1917.* Columbia, Mo.: University of Missouri Press.

Fletcher, Marvin. 1974. "The Black Bicycle Corps." *Arizona and the West* 16 (Spring):219–32.

Flipper, Henry Ossian. 1878. *The Colored Cadet at West Point.* New York, N.Y.: Homer Lee & Company.

_____. 1963. *Negro Frontiersman: The Western Memoirs of Henry O. Flipper.* Edited by Theodore D. Harris. El Paso, Tx.: Texas Western College Press.

Folsom, Franklin. 1973. *The Life and Legend of George McJunkin.* Nashville, Tenn.: Thomas Nelson.

Foner, Jack D. 1974. *Blacks and the Military in American History.* New York, N.Y.: Praeger.

Fowler, Arlen L. 1971. *The Black Infantry in the West, 1869–1891.* Westport, Conn.: Greenwood Publishing.

Fox, Stephen R. 1970. *The Guardian of Boston.* New York, N.Y.: Athenaeum.

Franklin, William E. 1963. "The Archy Case: The California Supreme Court Refuses to Free a Slave." *Pacific Historical Review* 32:137–54.

Frazier, Franklin E. 1963. *The Negro Church in America.* New York, N.Y.: Schocken Books.

Frost, Lawrence. 1986. *Custer's 7th Cavalry and the Campaign of 1873.* El Segundo, Calif.: Upton and Sons.

Good, Kenneth G. 19784. *California's Black Pioneers.* Santa Barbara, Calif.: McNall and Loftin.

Grafe, Willis R. 1991. *An Oregon Boy in the Yukon: A Story of the Alaska Highway.* Albany, Ore.: Chesnimus Press.

Graham, W. A. 1963. *The Custer Myth: A Sourcebook of Custeriana.* New York, N.Y.: Bonanza Books.

Greene, Robert E. 1974. *Black Defenders of America, 1775–1973.* Chicago, Ill.: Johnson Publishing.

Greer, Richard A. 1977. Honolulu in 1838. *The Hawai'ian Journal of History* 11:3–26.

Haley, James Evetts, ed. 1992. *Cowboys who Rode Proudly.* (Monograph.) Midland, Tx.: Nita Stewart Haley Memorial Library.

Hamilton, Kenneth M. 1991. *Black Towns and Profit.* Urbana and Chicago, Ill.: University of Illinois Press.

Hanes, Bailey C. 1977. *Bill Pickett*. Norman, Okla.: University of Oklahoma Press.

Hardaway, Roger D. 1995. *A Narrative Bibliography of the African-American Frontier*. Lampeter, Dyfed, Wales: United Kingdom.

Harndorff, Richard G. 1991. *Lakota Recollections of the Custer Fight: New Sources of Indian-Military History*. Spokane, Wash.: Arthur H. Clark Company.

Harrison, Edward S. 1905. *Nome and the Seward Peninsula: History, Description, Biographies, and Stories*. Seattle, Wash.: The Metropolitan Press.

Hausler, Donald. 1987. *Blacks in Oakland, 1852–1987*. Oakland, Calif.: Donald Hausler.

Haydon, Henry E., ed. 1891. *Poems on Alaska, the Land of the Midnight Sun*. By Authors Residing in the Territory. Sitka, Alaska: Alaska Press.

Hayes, Isaac Israel. 1874. *The Open Polar Sea: A Narrative of a Voyage of Discovery toward the North Pole in the Schooner "United States"*. New York, N.Y.: Hurd and Houghton.

_____. 1881. *Pictures of Arctic Travel*. New York, N.Y.: J.J. Little.

Henson, Josiah. 1849. *The Life of Josiah Henson, Formerly a Slave, Now an Inhabitant of Canada—as Narrated by Himself*. Boston, Mass.: Arthur D. Phelps.

Higginson, Thomas Wentworth. [1870] 1960. *Army Life in a Black Regiment*. Reprint, East Lansing: Michigan State University Press.

Hodges, Graham Russell. 1997. *Slavery and Freedom in the Rural North*. Madison, Wisc.: Madison House Publishers.

Holdredge, Helen. 1953. *Mammy Pleasant*. New York, N.Y.: G. P. Putnam's Sons.

Holmes, Edward, Jr. 1984. "A Brief Review of Black Cowboys in the Territory of Arizona." Ms. Arizona Historical Foundation, University of Arizona, Phoenix.

Holmes, Lewis. 1857. *The Arctic Whalemen*. Boston, Mass.: Wentworth and Company.

Hoy, Jim. 1986. Black Cowboys. *Kansas* 18 (November):48–50.

Hunt, Frazier, and Robert Hunt. 1947. *"I Fought with Custer": The Story of Sergeant Windolph*. New York: Charles Scribner's Sons.

Innis, Benjamin. 1973. *Bloody Knife: Custer's Favorate Scout*. Fort Collins, Colo.: Old Army Press.

Jacobs, Harriet A. 1987. *Incidents in the Life of a Slave Girl*. Edited by Jean Fagan Yellin. Cambridge, Mass.: Harvard University Press.

Jeltz, Wyatt F. 1948. The Relations of Negroes and Choctaws and Chickasaw Indians. *Journal of Negro History* 33:24–37.

Johnston, Hugh. 1984. *Canada's Ethnic Groups: The East Indians in Canada*. Booklet no. 5. Ottawa: Canadian Historical Association.

Johnston, Samuel P., ed. 1940. *Alaska Commercial Company, 1868–1940*. San Francisco, Calif.: E. E. Wachter, Printer.

Jones, Howard. 1987. *Mutiny on the Amistad*. New York, N.Y.: Oxford University Press.

Jordan, Bob. (n.d.) *Rodeo History and Legends*. Montrose, Colo.: Rodeo Stuff.

Kaplan, Sidney. 1973. *The Black Presence in the Era of the American Revolution, 1770–1800*. Washington, D.C.: Smithsonian Institution.

Katz, William L. 1971. *The Black West*. Garden City, N.Y.: Doubleday.

_____. 1995. *Black Women of the Old West*. New York, N.Y.: Atheneum Books for Young Readers.

_____. 1969. *Eyewitness: The Negro in American History*. New York, N.Y.: Pitman Publishing.

Kesey, Ken. 1994. *Last Go Round* (a novel). New York, N.Y.: Viking Books.

Langellier, John P. 1995. *Men A-Marching: The African American Soldier in the West, 1866–1896*. Springfield, Pa.: Steven Wright Publishing.

_____, and Alan Osur. 1980. *Chaplain Allen Allensworth and the 24th Infantry, 1886–1906*. Tucson, Ariz.: Tucson Corral of the Westerners.

Lapp, Rudolph M. 1966. Negro Rights Activities in Gold Rush California. *California Historical Society Quarterly* 45 (1):3–20.

_____. 1977. *Blacks in Gold Rush California*. New Haven, Conn.: Yale University Press.

Lasartemay, Eugene Pascal. n.d. "Jennie Daphne Prentiss: The Surrogate Mother of Jack London." Ms. Northern California Center for Afro American History and Life, Oakland.

Lautenschlager, Virginia. n.d. *Mary, the Custer Family Cook*. Ms. Hot Springs, S.D.

Leckie, William A. 1967. *The Buffalo Soldiers: A Narrative of the Negro Cavalry in the West*. Norman: University of Oklahoma Press.

Leonard, David W. 1995. *Delayed Frontier: The Peace River Country to 1909*. Calgary, Alberta, Canada: Detselig Enterprises, Ltd.

_____, and Victoria L. Lemieux. 1992. *The Lure of the Peace River Country*. Calgary, Alberta, Canada: Detselig Enterprises, Ltd.

Lewis, Meriweather. 1893. *History of the Expedition under the Command of Lewis and Clark to the Sources of the Missouri River*. 7 vols. New York, N.Y.: Francis P. Harper.

_____. 1904. *Original Journals of the Lewis and Clark Expedition, 1804–1806*. New York, N.Y.: Dodd, Mead and Company.

Libby, O. G., ed. 1973. *The Arikara Narrative of the Campaign against the Hostile Dakotas, June 1876*. New York, N.Y.: Solomon Lewis.

Limerick, Patricia Nelson, and Clyde A. Milner II, and Charles E. Rawkins.

1991. *Trails: Toward a New Western History*. Lawrence: University Press of Kansas.

Lobban, Richard A., Jr. 1995. *Cape Verde: Crioulo Colony to Independent Nation*. Boulder, Colo.: Westview Press.

Logan, Rayford W., and Michael R. Winston, eds. 1982. *Dictionary of American Negro Biography*. New York, N.Y.: Norton.

Long, Richard A. 1985. *Black Americana*. Secaucus, N.J.: Chartwell Books

Love, Nat. 1907. *The Life and Adventures of Nat Love, Better Known in the Cattle Country as "Deadwood Dick," by Himself*. Los Angeles, Calif.: Wayside Press.

McLagan, Elizabeth. 1980. *A Peculier Paradise*. The Oregon Black History Project. Portland, Ore.: The Georgian Press.

Manion, Mae. 1970. *"Prairie Pioneers" of Box Butte County*. Alliance, Nebr.: Iron Man Industries.

Maraniss, David. 1991. Buffalo Soldiers. *Washington Post*, January 20 issue.

Markham, Sir Albert Hastings. 1875. *A Whaling Cruise to Baffin's Bay and the Gulf of Boothia*. London, England: S. Low, Marston, Low and Searle.

Markle, Donald E. 1994. *Spies and Spymasters of the Civil War*. New York, N.Y.: Barnes and Noble.

Maur, Geoffrey. n.d. "Blacks of Phoenix, 1890–1930." Ms. Arizona Historical Foundation, University of Arizona, Phoenix.

Micheaux, Oscar. 1913. *The Conquest: The Story of a Negro Pioneer* (a novel). Lincoln, Nebr.: Woodruff.

_____. 1915. *The Forged Note: A Romance of the Darker Races*. Lincoln, Nebr.: Western Book Supply.

_____. 1917. *The Homesteader* (a novel). College Park, Md.: McGrath Publishing.

_____. 1941. *The Wind from Nowhere* (a novel). New York, N.Y.: Book Supply.

Middleton, Stephen. 1993. *The Black Laws in the Old Northwest*. Westport, Conn.: Greenwood Press.

Miller, Edward A. 1995. *Gullah Statesmen: Robert Smalls from Slavery to Congress, 1839–1915*. Columbia: University of South Carolina Press.

Montesano, Phil. 1969. A Black Pioneer's Trip to California. *Pacific Historian* 13 (Winter):58–62.

Mulroy, Kevin. 1993. *Freedom on the Border: The Seminole Maroons in Florida, the Indian Territory, Coahila, and Texas*. Lubbock: Texas Tech University Press.

Mumford, Esther Hall. 1981. *Seattle's Black Victorians, 1852–1901*. Seattle, Wash.: Ananse Press.

Museum of Modern Art. 1966. *The Hampton Album*. New York, N.Y.: Museum of Modern Art.

The Negroes of Nebraska. 1940. WPA Project. Lincoln, Nebr.: Woodruff Printing.

Newgard, Thomas, and William Sherman. n.d. *Plain Folks: North Dakota Ethnic History.* Fargo: North Dakota State University Press.

_____, _____, and John Guerrero. 1994. *African Americans in North Dakota.* Bismarck, N.D.: University of Mary Press.

Newman, Debra L., comp. 1984. *Black History: A Guide to Civilian Records in the Nation Archives.* Washington, D.C.: National Archives Trust Fund Board.

Nordyke, Eleanor C. 1988. Blacks in Hawai'i: A Demographic and Historical Perspective. *The Hawai'ian Journal of History* 22:241–55.

Ogden, George Washington. 1905. Letters from the West, 1821. In *Early Western Travels, 1748–1846.* Vol. 19. Edited by Ruben Gold Thwaites. Cleveland, Ohio: Arthur H. Clark Company.

Olcione, Amos, and Thomas Senter, eds. 1996. *Kenneth Wiggins Porter's "The Black Seminoles: A History of a Freedom-Seeking People."* Gainesville, Fla.: University Press of Florida.

Oliver, Mamie O. 1990. *Idaho Ebony: The Afro-American Present in Idaho State History.* Boise, Idaho: Idaho Centennial Foundation, Inc.

Organ, Claude H., ed. 1987. *A Century of Black Surgeons.* Norman, Okla.: Transcript Press.

Overstreet, Everett Louis. 1990. *Black on a Background of White: A Chronicle of Afro-Americans' Involvement in America's Last Frontier, Alaska.* Anchorage: Alaska Black Caucus.

Palmer, Howard, and Tamara Palmer. 1985. *Peoples of Alberta.* Saskatoon, Saskatchewan, Canada: Western Producer Prairie Books.

Painter, Nell Irvin. 1977. *Exodusters: Black Migration to Kansas after Reconstruction.* New York, N.Y.: Knopf.

Papanikolas, Helen Z., ed. 1981. *The Peoples of Utah.* Salt Lake City: Utah State Historical Society.

Petrov, Ivan. 1884. *Report on the Population, Industries, and Resources of Alaska.* Washington, D.C.: U.S. Government Printing Office.

Ploski, Harry A., and James Williams, eds. 1989. *The Negro Almanac: A Reference Work on the African American.* Detroit, Mich.: Gale Research.

Polz, Ruth. 1990. *Black Heroes of the Wild West.* Seattle, Wash.: Open Hand Publishing.

Porter, Kenneth Wiggins. 1996. *The Negro on the American Frontier.* Edited by John W. "Jack" Ravage. Stratford, New Hampshire: Ayer Publishers.

Ravage, John W. "Jack." 1991. *Singletree* (a novel). Laramie, Wyo.: Jelm Mountain Publications.

_____. 1992. "Blacks in the American West." *History of Photography* 16 (Winter):392–96.

Remington, Frederic. 1960. *Frederick Remington's Own West*. Edited by Harold McCracken. New York, N.Y.: Dial Press.

Rhode Island Black Heritage Society. N.d. *Creative Survival: The Providence Black Community in the 19th Century*. Providence, R.I.: Rhode Island Black Heritage Society.

Richardson, Marilyn. 1987. *Maria W. Stewart: America's First Black Woman Political Writer*. Bloomington: Indiana University Press.

Robbins, A. C. 1883. *Legacy to Buxton*. Chatham, Ontario, Canada: Ideal Printing.

Robinson, Charles M., III. 1991. The Whirlwind and His Scouts. *Old West* 28 (Summer):28–37.

Robinson, Gwendolyn, and John W. Robinson. 1989. *Seek the Truth*. Chatham, Ontario, Canada: Gwendolyn Robinson and John W. Robinson.

Roosevelt, Theodore. 1899. *The Rough Riders*. New York, N.Y.: Charles Scribner's Sons.

Roper, Stephanie Abbot. 1994. From Military Forts to "Nigger Towns": African Americans in North Dakota, 1890–1940. *Heritage of the Great Plains* 27 (1):27–53.

Rusco, Elmer R. 1975. *Good Times Coming? Black Nevadans in the Nineteenth Century*. Westport, Conn.: Greenwood Press.

Sackinger, Patricia. 1974. Research project in Black history. Ms. Archives and Manuscript Collection, University of Alaska at Fairbanks, December.

Sammons, Vivian Ovelton. 1990. *Blacks in Science and Medicine*. New York, N.Y.: Hemisphere Publishing.

Savage, Sherwood. 1976. *Blacks in the West*. Westport, Conn.: Greenwood Press.

_____. 1994. *On the Trail of the Buffalo Soldier: Biographies of African-American Soldiers, 1868–1918*. Wilmington, Del.: Scholarly Resources.

Savage, W. Sherman. 1940a. The Negro in the Western Movement. *Journal of Negro History* 25:531–39.

_____. 1940b. The Negro on the Mining Frontier. *Journal of Negro History* 30:30–46.

_____. 1951. The Role of Negro Soldiers in Protecting the Indian Territory from Intruders. *Journal of Negro History* 35:25–34.

Schmitt, Robert C. 1980. Some Firsts in Island Business and Government. *The Hawai'ian Journal of History* 14:80–97.

Schubert, Frank N. 1970. The Black Regular Army Regiments in Wyoming,

1885–1912. Masters thesis, University of Wyoming, Laramie.

_____. 1974. The Fort Robinson YMCA. *Nebraska History* 55 (Summer):165–79.

_____. 1974. The Violent World of Emanuel Stance. *Nebraska History* 55 (Summer):203–19.

_____. 1977. *Fort Robinson, Nebraska: The History of a Military Community, 1874–1916*. Ph.D. diss. Ann Arbor, Mich: University Microfilms International.

_____. 1993. *Buffalo Soldiers, Braves and the Brass*. Shippensburg Penn.: White Mane Publishing Company.

Scoresby, Captain. 1820. *The Arctic Regions and the Northern Whale-Fishery*. London, England: The Religious Tract Society.

Shaw, James C. 1952. *North from Texas: Incidents in the Early Life of a Range Cowman in Texas, Dakota, and Wyoming, 1852—1880*. Evanston, Ill.: Branding Iron Press.

Shepard, R. Bruce. 1985. Plain Racism: The Reaction against Oklahoma Black Immigraton to the Canadian Plains. *Prairie Forum* 10 (Autumn):114–21.

Shirley, Glenn. 1962. *Heck Thomas, Frontier Marshall: The Story of a Real Gunfighter*. New York, N.Y.: Chilton Book Division.

_____. 1957. *Law West of Forth Smith*. New York, N.Y.: Henry Holt.

Shreve, Dorothy Shadd. 1983. *The AfriCanadian Church: A Stabilizer*. Jordan Station, Ontario, Canada: Paidea Press.

Siebert, Wilbur Henry. 1898. *The Underground Railroad from Slavery to Freedom*. New York, N.Y.: MacMillan.

Siringo, Charles. 1927. *Riata and Spurs*. Boston, Mass.: Houghton, Mifflin Co.

Simpson, MacKinnon, and Robert B. Goodman. 1986. *Whale Song: The Story of Hawai'i and the Whales*. Honolulu, Hawaii: Beyond Words Publishing Company.

Smith, Gloria. 1977. *Black Americana in Arizona*. Tucson, Ariz.: Gloria L. Smith.

Smith, Herndon, ed. 1942. *Centralia: The First Fifty Years, 1845–1900*. Rochester, Wash.: Gorham Printing.

Smith, Jessie Carney, ed. 1991. *Notable Black American Women*. Detroit, Mich.: Gale Research.

Stampp, Kenneth Milton. 1956. *The Peculiar Institution: Slavery in the Ante-Bellum South*. New York, N.Y.: Knopf.

Stark, Sylvia. 1993. *Sylvia Stark: A Pioneer*. Seattle, Wash.: Open Hand Publishing.

Stewart, Paul W. 1976. *Westward Soul*. Denver, Colo.: Black American West Foundation.

_____, and Wallace Young Ponce. 1986. *Black Cowboys*. Denver, Colo.: Black American West Museum and Heritage Center.

Steward, Theophilus Gould. 1904. *The Colored Regulars in the United States Army*. Philadelphia, Pa.: A.M.E. Book Concern.

Stover, Earl F. 1971. Chaplain Henry V. Plummer: His Ministry and His Court Martial. *Nebraska History* 56 (Spring):20–50.

Struhsaker, Virginia L. 1975. Stockton's Black Pioneers. *Pacific Historian* 19 (Winter):347–54.

_____. 1977. Doc Shadd. *Saskatchewan History* 30 (Spring):42–46.

Talmadge, Marian, and Iris Gilmore. 1973. *Barney Ford, Black Baron*. New York, N.Y.: Dodd, Mead and Company.

Thompson, Stith, ed. 1935. *Round the Levee*. Austin, Tx: Texas Folk-Lore Society.

Thomson, Colin A. 1979. *Blacks in Deep Snow: Black Pioneers in Canada*. Don Mills, Ontario, Canada: J. M. Dent & Sons.

Thum, Marcella. 1992. *Hippocrene USA Guide to Black America*. New York, N.Y.: Hippocrene Books.

Thurman, A. Odell. 1975. The Negro in California before 1890. *Pacific Historian* 19 (Winter):321–46.

Thurman, Sue Bailey. 1952. *Pioneers of Negro Origin in California*. San Francisco, Calif.: Acme Publishing.

Thwaites, Reuben Gold, ed. 1905. *Early Western Travels, 1748–1846*. Cleveland, Ohio: Arthur H. Clark Company.

Tolson, Arthur L. 1974. *The Black Oklahomans: A History, 1541-1972*. New Orleans, La.: Edwards Printing.

Tompkins, E. 1972. Black Ahab: William T. Shorey, Whaling Master. *California Historical Quarterly* 51 (Spring):75–84.

Trivelli, Marifrances. 1995. "I Knew a Ship from Stem to Stern": The Maritime World of Frederick Douglass. *The Log of the Mystic Seaport* 46 (4):98–108.

Turner, Frederick Jackson. [1929] 1986. *The Frontier in American History*. Reprint, Tucson, Ariz.: University of Arizona Press

Utendale, Kent Alan. 1985. Race Relations in Canada's Midwest: A Study of the Immigration, Integration, and Assimilation of Black Minority Groups. Ph.D. diss. Pacific Western University, Vancouver, British Columbia, Canada.

VanDeburg, William L. 1984. *Slavery and Race in American Popular Culture*. Madison: University of Wisconsin Press.

Van Deusen, John. 1936. The Exodus of 1879. *Journal of African American History* 21:111–29.

Vestal, Stanley. 1956. *Sitting Bull: Champion of the Sioux*. Norman: University of Oklahoma Press.

Victoria Black People's Society. 1978. *Blacks in British Columbia: A Catalog of Information and Sources of Information Pertaining to Blacks in British Columbia*. Victoria, British Columbia, Canada: Victoria Black People's Society.

Walhouse, Freda. 1961. *The Influence of Minority Ethnic Groups on the Cultural Geography of Vancouver*. Vancouver, British Columbia, Canada: University of British Columbia Archives, Special Collections.

Walker, James W. St. G. n.d. *Canada's Ethnic Groups: The West Indians in Canada*. Publication no. 6. Ottawa, Ontario: Canadian Historical Association.

Washington, Booker T. 1909. *The Story of the Negro: The Rise of the Race from Slavery*. 2 vols. New York, N.Y.: Peter Smith.

Washington State Library. 1970. *The Negro in the State of Washington, 1788–1969: A Bibliography of Published and of Unpublished Source Materials on the Life and Achievements of the Negro in the Evergreen State*. Rev. ed. Olympia, Wash.: Washington State Library.

Welsh, Donald H. 1953. Pierre Wilbaux, Cattle King. *North Dakota Journal of History* 20:5–23.

Wesley, Charles H., and Patricia Romero. 1967. *Negro Americans in the Civil War*. Vol. 3 of the International Library of Negro Life and History. New York, N.Y.: Publisher's Company, Inc.

Wharfield, H. B. 1965. *10th Cavalry and Border Fights*. El Cajon, Calif.: H. B. Wharfield.

White, E. E. 1965. *Experience of a Special Indian Agent*. Norman: University of Oklahoma Press.

White, Sid, and S. E. Solberg, eds. 1989. *Peoples of Washington: Perspectives on Cultural Diversity*. Pullman: Washington State University Press.

Whitman, Sidney E. 1962. *The Troopers: An Informal History of the Plains Cavalry, 1865–1890*. New York, N.Y.: Hastings House.

Wight, Willard E., ed. 1956. A Young Medical Officer's Letters from Fort Robinson and Fort Leavenworth, 1905–1907. *Nebraska History* 37:135–47.

Willey, Austin. [1860] 1969. *The History of the Anti-Slavery Cause in State and Nation*. Reprint, New York, N.Y.: Negro Universities Press.

Williams, Gerald O. 1988. *Michael J.* [i.e., A.] *Healy and the Alaska Maritime Frontier, 1880–1902*. Ph.D. diss. Ann Arbor, Mich.: University Microfilms International.

Williams, Jennie Winona. 1942. Allen and Winona Williams: Pioneers of Sheridan and Johnson Counties. *Annals of Wyoming* 14:193–99.

Williams, Mildred. 1990. An Historical Sketch of the Development of the Black

Church in America and in Oakland, California. Masters thesis, Bay City Bible Institute, San Francisco, California.

Williams, Nudie Engene. 1973. Black United States Marshall in the Territory, 1875–1907. Masters thesis, Oklahoma State University, Stillwater, Okla.

_____. 1981. Black Men Who Wore the "Star." *Chronicles of Oklahoma* 59 (Spring):83–90.

_____. 1987. Black Political Patronage in the Western District of Arkansas, 1871–1892. *Journal of the Fort Smith Historical Society* 11 (September):5–8.

Willis, Deborah. 1993. *J.P. Ball, Daguerrean and Studio Photographer.* New York, N.Y.: Garland Publishing Co.

_____. 1985. *Black Photographers, 1840–1940.* New York, N.Y.: Garland Publishers, Inc.

Winks, Robin W. 1971. *The Blacks in Canada: A History.* Montreal, Quebec, Canada: McGill-Queen's University Press.

Wood, A. B. 1938. The Coad Brothers: Panhandle Cattle Kings. *Nebraska History* 19:28–43.

Woodson, Carter G. 1922. *The Negro in Our History.* Washington, D.C.: The Associated Publishers, Inc.

Wright, Donald R. 1993. *African Americans in the Early Republic.* Arlington Heights, Ill.: Harlan Davidson, Inc.

Yellin, Jean Fagan, and Cynthia D. Bond. 1991. *The Pen Is Ours: A List of Writings by and about African American Women before 1910 with Secondary Bibliography to the Present.* New York, N.Y.: Oxford University Press.

INDEX